Jumpers

Tom Stoppard's other work includes: *Enter a Free Man, Rosencrantz and Guildenstern Are Dead, The Real Inspector Hound, Jumpers, Travesties, Night and Day, Every Good Boy Deserves Favour* (with Andre Previn), *After Magritte, Dirty Linen, The Real Thing, Hapgood, Arcadia, Indian Ink* and *The Invention of Love*. His radio plays include: *If You're Glad, I'll Be Frank, Albert's Bridge, Where Are They Now?, Artist Descending a Staircase, The Dog It Was That Died* and *In the Native State*. Work for television includes *Professional Foul* and *Squaring the Circle*. His film credits include *Empire of the Sun, Rosencrantz and Guildenstern Are Dead*, which he also directed, *Shakespeare in Love* (with Marc Norman) and *Enigma*.

TOM STOPPARD

Jumpers

faber and faber

First published in 1972 by
Faber and Faber Limited
3 Queen Square London WCIN 3AU
This revised edition first published in 1986

Photoset by Wilmaset, Birkenhead, Wirral
Printed and bound in Great Britain by
Mackays of Chatham PLC, Chatham, Kent
All rights reserved

All rights whatsoever in this play are strictly reserved and
professional application to perform it, etc., must be made
in advance, before rehearsals begin, to Fraser and Dunlop (Scripts) Ltd,
5th Floor, The Chambers, Chelsea Harbour, Lots Road, London SW10 0XF,
and amateur applications for permission to perform, etc., must be made
in advance, before rehearsals begin, to Samuel French Ltd,
52 Fitzroy Street, London WIP 6JR

A CIP record for this book is
available from the British Library

ISBN 0–571–14569–8

12 14 16 18 20 19 17 15 13

Author's Note

This new edition of *Jumpers* incorporates some changes, mostly small but too numerous to specify, made for the 1984 production at the Aldwych Theatre, London. The original production and the two revivals were directed by Peter Wood to whom I reiterate my thanks for encouraging my inconvenient habit (inconvenient to my publishers) of treating rehearsals as an opportunity to revise the text: the most notable result on this occasion was the re-introduction, in the Coda, of Captain Scott, who appeared in the first edition but not in the second, and of Tarzan who swung out of view after the first few previews in 1972 and is here making his début in print.

The new production was presented by Michael Codron with the following cast:

GEORGE	Paul Eddington
DOROTHY	Felicity Kendal
ARCHIE	Simon Cadell
BONES	Andrew Sachs
CROUCH	Timothy Bateson
SECRETARY	Gail Rolfe
MCFEE	Paul Tomkinson
JUMPERS etc.	Lenny Bickley
	Justin Church
	Nigel Johnson
	Colin Orr
	Jeffrey Pepper
	Roy Rowlands
	Carl Toop
	Philip Tsaras
	Donald Waugh
Directed by	Peter Wood
Designed by	Carl Toms
Lighting by	David Hersey
Movement by	David Toguri

There are three playing areas, the study, the bedroom, and the hall.

There is also a screen, ideally forming a backdrop to the whole stage. Film and slides are to be back-projected on to this screen on a scale big enough to allow actors and furniture to mask the images without significantly obscuring them.

It is an essential requirement of the play that the bedroom can be blacked out completely while the action continues elsewhere.

For the purpose of the stage directions given hereafter, I am assuming the following layout.

The front door is Upstage Centre.

The study occupies the whole area stage left of the hall and front door.

The bedroom occupies the rest of the stage. If the rooms are on a 'revolve', they may dominate the playing-area in turn.

The apartment belongs to GEORGE, a Professor of Moral Philosophy, married to a prematurely-retired musical-comedy actress of some renown, DOROTHY. The general standard of living suggested by the flat owes more, one would guess, to musical comedy than moral philosophy, and this is especially true of the bedroom which is lushly carpeted and includes among its furnishings a television set remotely-controlled by an electronic portable switch; a record player; two elegant straight-backed chairs and one comfortable upholstered chair; a globular goldfish-bowl containing one goldfish; and a four-poster bed which can be enclosed at will by the drapes adorning its corners. The effect is elegant, feminine, expensive. The bedroom has two doors, one leading into the wings at Stage Left (the unseen bathroom), and the second into the hall. This latter door must be sturdily fixed. It opens inwards, the hinges upstage, so that when this door is wide open the inside of it is hidden from the audience. The room also has a french window, guarded on the exterior by a mock-balcony or balustrade; it overlooks streets and sky for the flat is in an upper floor of a big old-fashioned but newly redecorated and converted mansion.

The study may contain a day-bed against the upstage wall,

7

bookshelves above the bed, a desk and chair for the Secretary, and a bigger desk for George. On the wings-side of the room is a tall cupboard or wardrobe. The room contains, somewhere, a tape-recorder; a bow and quiver of arrows, together with an archery target about a yard in diameter; an electric typewriter for the Secretary to use; a smallish wooden box such as a small tortoise might live in, and a large wooden box such as a rabbit might live in. There is a door into the hall. George's desk, when we discover it, is a clutter of books and manuscript.

However, none of the above is visible for the first few minutes of the play, for which is required an empty space. . . .

THE CHARACTERS

GEORGE *is between 40 and 50, and still attractive enough to make it perfectly plausible that he should be married to* DOTTY *who is ten to fifteen years younger and very beautiful indeed.*

ARCHIE *is a dandy.*

INSPECTOR BONES *is middle-aged and carelessly dressed.*

CROUCH *is old and small and a bit stooped.*

The SECRETARY *is young and attractive but poker-faced, almost grim, even on her first appearance, in which she performs as a stripper.*

The JUMPERS *are dressed in yellow uniforms – tracksuit trousers and singlets – and although they pass muster at first glance, they are not as universally youthful or athletic-looking as one might expect.*

ACT ONE

ARCHIE: (*Unseen*) And now, ladies and gentlemen, on the occasion of a momentous Radical Liberal victory at the polls, may I present your hostess and mine, making a most welcome reappearance, the much-missed, much-loved star of the musical stage, the incomparable, magnetic Dorothy Moore! (DOTTY *enters. Much applause.*)

DOTTY: Thank you, thank you for coming. (*To* PIANO PLAYER) Thank you, Sam.
(*Music introduction for* 'Shine on Harvest Moon'. *She dries. Introduction repeated.*)
How does it begin?
(GUESTS, *offstage, sing* 'Shine on, shine on harvest moon'.)
(*Singing, but going wrong immediately.*)
I want to spoon to my honey I'll croon love's June or July.
(*Breaks off.*) No I can't. I'm sorry (*and goes*).
(*Drum roll.*)

Cries of disappointment change to cries of delight.
Like a pendulum between darkness and darkness, the
SECRETARY *swings into the spotlight, and out. She is on a swing, making an arc from wing to wing, in sight for a second, out of sight for a second, in sight for a second, out of sight for a second . . . back and forth. The swing itself hangs from a chandelier.*
Cheers.
Each time she reappears she has taken off some clothing.
Grateful cheers.
CROUCH *enters from side, the porter pressed into service to serve drinks at the party. He wears a short white coat and carries a round tray balanced on one hand, drinks on tray.*
He is going to stray into the line of vision. Voices warn him away, good-humouredly.
CROUCH *does not know what is going on: every time he turns downstage, the* SECRETARY *is in view behind him, and every time he looks upstage the gap is empty.*

9

There is the sound of the GUESTS . . .

'Mind your back!'

'Out the way!'

'Let the dog see the rabbit!'

CROUCH *is bewildered.*

The SECRETARY *is nearing nakedness, obscured. The unseen
watchers are nearing hysterical frustration.*

At the climax of their cries, CROUCH *backs into the path of the
swing and is knocked arse over tip by a naked lady.* BLACK-
OUT *and crash of broken glass. Immediately:* GEORGE *and a
telephone in a spotlight.*

GEORGE: (*On telephone*) Could I speak to the Chief Inspector or
someone in authority? . . . Well, Constable, I'd like to
make a complaint about a disturbance of the peace at – I'd
prefer it to be an anonymous complaint. Well, do you
accept pseudonymous complaints? . . . Never mind, my
name is Wittgenstein and the party – the guilty party in fact
is at – What? Oh, good God – 'W' as in Wagner, 'I' as in id
. . . no *I D* – 'I', 'D' as in dog . . . bow-wow . . . (*Blackout
on* GEORGE.)

VOICE: (*Archie's voice*) 'And now! – ladies and gentlemen! – the
INCREDIBLE – RADICAL! – LIBERAL!! – JUMPERS!!'
(*White spot. Musical introduction.*

THE JUMPERS *enter jumping, tumbling, somersaulting, four from
each side of the stage: a not especially talented troupe of gymnasts.
Discreet musical accompaniment.*

*Their separate entrances converge to form a tableau of modest
pretension.*)

DOTTY: (*Entering*) That's not incredible. . . . Well, is it? I can sing
better than that. I mean I can sing better than they can jump.
(DOTTY *wanders on to the stage in front of the now
disassembling tableau. Her blonde hair is elegantly 'up', her
white dress is long and billowy . . . she looks fabulous,
stunning. She flaps a hand dismissively at the* JUMPERS.)
(*Equably.*) No good – you're still credible. (*Generally.*) Get
me someone unbelievable!
(GEORGE, *holding sheets of paper, has already entered behind
her.*)

GEORGE: Dotty!

    (GEORGE *is not dressed for a party. Flannels and shabby
    smoking jacket, hair awry, his expression and manner signifying
    remonstrance. The* JUMPERS *persevere, doggedly helping each
    other to do back-flips, etc.*)

DOTTY: I have a complaint. These people are supposed to be
    incredible and I'm not even astonished. *I am not faintly
    surprised.* In fact, not only can I sing better than they can
    jump, I can probably jump higher than they can sing.

GEORGE: For God's sake. It's after two a.m.

    (GEORGE *goes as far as to touch her arm. She turns on him with
    sudden obliterating fury.*)

DOTTY: It's my bloody party, George!

GEORGE: What if someone phones the police?

DOTTY: They can come too. (*To the piano*) Give me an A.

    (GEORGE *leaves.*)

    (*A* JUMPER *flips himself into a standing position in mid-stage.*)

    (*Equable again.*) I can do that.

    (*A* SECOND JUMPER *joins the first.*)

    And that.

    (*A* THIRD JUMPER *leaps on to the shoulders of the first two.*)

    I can't do that, but my belief is unshakeable, so get off.

    (*To the unseen musicians.*) I'll do the one about the moon. I'm
    sure you know it.

    (*A word about Dotty's song. The musicians attempt to follow her
    but are thwarted by her inability to distinguish between one
    moon-song and another, and by her habit of singing the words of
    one to the tune of another. The music gamely keeps switching
    tracks, but* DOTTY *keeps double-crossing it.*)

    (*Sings*) Shine on, shine on silvery moon
        I used to sigh
        In June or July
        How high the –
        moon, you saw me standing alone –
    (*The last six words have fortuitously combined the words and
    tune of* 'Blue Moon'.)
    That's it, that's it!

(Now confident, she starts to play the chanteuse, *strolling in and out among the dogged* JUMPERS, *moving upstage of them and turning.)*

(Sings) Blue moon
    You saw me standing alone
    Without a dream in my heart
    It must have been moonglow
    Way up in the Blue Moon

(From now until their act is terminated by events, the JUMPERS *are assembling themselves into a human pyramid. When the pyramid is complete it hides* DOTTY *from view.)*

(Sings) You saw me standing in June
    January, Allegheny, Moon or July –

(Jeers.) Jumpers I've *had* – yellow, I've had them all! *In*credible, *barely* credible, credible and all too bloody likely – When I say jump, *jump!*
(From her tone now it should be apparent that DOTTY, *who may have appeared pleasantly drunk, is actually breaking up mentally. And from her position in the near-dark outside the* JUMPERS' *light, it should be possible to believe that* DOTTY *is responsible for what happens next – which is: A gun shot.* ONE JUMPER *is blown out of the pyramid. He falls downstage, leaving the rest of the pyramid intact. The music has stopped.* DOTTY, *chanteuse, walks through the gap in the pyramid. The shot* JUMPER *is at her feet. He starts to move, dying, pulling himself up against* DOTTY's *legs. She looks at him in surprise as he crawls up her body. His blood is on her dress. She holds him under his arms, and looks around in a bewildered way. She whimpers.)*
Archie . . .
(The pyramid has been defying gravity for these few seconds. Now it slowly collapses into the dark, imploding on the missing part, and rolling and separating, out of sight, leaving only the white spot.

The party hubbub comes back, at a higher pitch. DOTTY *does not move, holding the* JUMPER.)

ARCHIE: (*Voice only*) . . . Quiet please. . . . the party is over . . .

A DRUNK: (*Sings*) It's time to call it a day . . .

(This sets off a ripple of applause and cheers.
The party noise dies to silence.
The light contracts to a spot on DOTTY *and the* JUMPER, *eerily.*
Frozen time. DOTTY *still has not moved. Around her the bed-*
room has assembled. ARCHIE *appears in the bedroom.*)

DOTTY: Archie . . .

ARCHIE: Oh dear.

DOTTY: It's Duncan.

ARCHIE: Yes – poor McFee.

DOTTY: Archie . . .

ARCHIE: There's no need to get it out of proportion. Death is always a great pity of course but it's not as though the alternative were immortality.

DOTTY: Archie . . .

ARCHIE: Just keep him out of sight till morning. I'll be back.

DOTTY: Archie . . .

ARCHIE: Hush. I'll be back at eight o'clock.

(ARCHIE *leaves.*)

(The white spot remains – on the screen now: but it is changing in
character, and becomes a map of the moon photographed from a
satellite . . . the familiar pitted circle. At the same time is heard
the low tone of the TELEVISION VOICE, *too low to admit*
comprehension. The picture changes to a close up of the moon's
surface. It is morning. We are watching a television programme
about something that has happened on the moon.
The picture changes several times – an astronaut, a rocket, a
moon-vehicle, etc.
The television set in the bedroom is on.
DOTTY *is standing in the bedroom. She hasn't moved at all. She*
is dressed in a blood-stained party frock, holding up a corpse
dressed in yellow trousers and singlet. She is looking about her,
clearly trying to decide what to do with the body.
In the study, GEORGE *is working at the desk, adding to a pile of*
manuscript.

The front door opens. CROUCH *enters, using a master key. He is not wearing the white coat now, but a grey overall as worn by janitors. He is limping slightly. He is singing quietly to himself* . . . 'Gonna make a sentimental journey . . . gonna put my heart at ease . . . gonna take a sentimental journey . . .' DOTTY *has heard him. She turns down the sound of the TV, using the remote control device.*)

DOTTY: . . . Archie . . . !

CROUCH: It's Crouch, madam.

(CROUCH *continues and exits to kitchen.*

DOTTY *sits down on the bed, the corpse slumped over her knees. She glances at the TV. She turns up the volume.*)

TV VOICE: — in a tight spot. And so in the crippled space capsule, Captain Scott is on his way back to earth, the first Englishman to reach the moon, but his triumph will be over-shadowed by the memory of Astronaut Oates, a tiny receding figure waving forlornly from the featureless wastes of the lunar landscape.

(DOTTY *changes the channel.*

On the screen: a big procession in the streets of London, military in tone (brass band music) but celebratory: for five seconds.

DOTTY *changes the channel.*

A commercial: for three seconds.

DOTTY *changes the channel.*

The Moon programme again.)

— which followed the discovery that the damage on impact had severely reduced the thrust of the rockets that are fired for take-off. Millions of viewers saw the two astronauts struggling at the foot of the ladder until Oates was knocked to the ground by his commanding officer . . . Captain Scott has maintained radio silence since pulling up the ladder and closing the hatch with the remark, 'I am going up now. I may be gone for some time.'

(DOTTY *changes channel. The procession on screen. Military music. She looks gloomily, helplessly at the corpse. She notes the blood on her dress. She takes the dress off.*

CROUCH *enters from the kitchen, carrying a bin of rubbish and several empty champagne bottles.*

DOTTY *hears the kitchen door. She turns the TV sound down low.*)

DOTTY: What time is it, Crouch?

CROUCH: Nearly nine o'clock, madam.

(CROUCH *leaves by the front door as the* SECRETARY *enters. The* SECRETARY *hurries in, in the act of taking off her overcoat and hat.*

CROUCH *lets himself out, closing the front door. The* SECRETARY *enters the study, closes the door behind her, hangs up her hat and coat in the wardrobe, sits down at her desk, and arranges her notebook and pencil.* GEORGE *has continued to write without looking up.*)

DOTTY: (*Very quietly*) Help! (*Slightly louder*) Help!

(GEORGE *looks up and stares thoughtfully at the audience. He looks down again and continues to write.*

The bedroom blacks out.

GEORGE *stops writing, gets to his feet. His system – for preparing lectures – is to scrawl them over many pieces of paper, which he then dictates to the* SECRETARY *who will type them out. He does not take much notice of the* SECRETARY.

GEORGE *now collects the pages into a tidy sheaf, assumes a suitable stance, and takes it from the top . . .*)

GEORGE: Secondly! . . .

(*He has ambushed himself. He looks around and retrieves the missing sheet from behind his desk.* GEORGE *takes up his stance anew.*)

To begin at the beginning –

DOTTY: (*Off. Panic.*) Help! Murder!

(GEORGE *throws his manuscript on to the desk and marches angrily to the door.*)

(*Off*) Oh, horror, horror, horror! Confusion now hath made its masterpiece . . . most sacrilegious murder! – (*Different voice.*) Woe, alas! What, in our house?

(GEORGE, *with his hand on the door handle, pauses. He returns to his desk and picks up his papers.*)

GEORGE: To begin at the beginning: Is God? (*Pause.*) I prefer to put the question in this form because to ask, 'Does God exist?' appears to presuppose the existence of a God who may not, and I do not propose this late evening to follow my friend Russell, this evening to follow my late friend Russell, to follow my good friend the late Lord Russell, necrophiliac rubbish!, to begin at the beginning: is God? (*He ponders a moment.*) To ask, 'Is God' appears to presuppose a Being who perhaps isn't . . . and thus is open to the same objection as the question, 'Does God exist?' . . . but until the difficulty is pointed out it does not have the same propensity to confuse language with meaning and to conjure up a God who may have any number of predicates including omniscience, perfection and four-wheel-drive but not, as it happens, existence. This confusion, which indicates only that language is an approximation of meaning and not a logical symbolism for it, began with Plato and was not ended by Bertrand Russell's theory that existence could only be asserted of descriptions and not of individuals, but I do not propose this evening to follow into the Theory of Descriptions my very old friend – now dead, of course – *ach!* – to follow into the Theory of Descriptions, the late Lord Russell – ! (*He continues smoothly, improvising off-script.*) – if I may so refer to an old friend for whom punctuality was no less a predicate than existence, and a good deal more so, he would have had us believe, though why we should believe that existence could be asserted of the author of 'Principia Mathematica' but not of Bertrand Russell, he never had time, despite his punctuality, not to mention his existence, to explain, very good, keep to the point, to begin at the beginning: *is God?* (*To* SECRETARY.) Leave a space. Secondly! A small number of men, by the exercise of their intellects and by the study of the works both of nature and of other intellects before them, have been able to argue coherently against the existence of God. A much larger number of men, by the exercise of their emotional and psychological states, have affirmed that this is the correct view. This view derives partly from what is known as common sense, whose virtue, uniquely among virtues, is that everybody has it, and partly from the mounting implausibility of a technological age as having divine origins – for while a man might believe that the providence of sheep's wool was made in heaven, he finds it harder to believe the same of Terylene mixture. Well, the tide is running his way, and it is a tide which has turned only once in human history. . . . There is presumably a calendar date – a *moment* – when the onus of proof passed from the atheist to the believer, when, quite suddenly, secretly, the noes had it. It is now nearly fifty years since Professor Ramsey described theology and ethics as two subjects without an object, and yet, as though to defy reason, as though to flaunt a divine indestructibility, the question will not go away: is God?

DOTTY: (*Off*) Rape!

GEORGE: And then again, I sometimes wonder whether the question ought not to be, 'Are God?' Because it is to account for two quite unconnected mysteries that the human mind looks beyond humanity and it is two of him that philosophy obligingly provides. There is, first, the God of Creation to account for existence, and, second, the God of Goodness to account for moral values. I say they are unconnected because there is no logical reason why the fountainhead of goodness in the universe should have necessarily created the universe in the first place; nor is it necessary, on the other hand, that a Creator should care tuppence about the behaviour of his creations. Still, at least in the Judaeo-Christian tradition, nothing is heard either of a God who created the universe and then washed his hands of it, or, alternatively, a God who merely took a comparatively recent interest in the chance product of universal gases. In practice, people admit a Creator to give authority to moral values, and admit moral values to give point to the Creation. But when we place the existence of God within the discipline of a philosophical inquiry, we find these two independent mysteries: the how and the why of the overwhelming question: –

DOTTY: (*Off*) *Is anybody there?*

GEORGE: (*Pause*) Quite.

(DOTTY *screams. It sounds in earnest. Of course, nothing can
be seen.*)

(*Murmurs*) Wolf. . . .

DOTTY: (*Off*) Wolves! – Look out!

(GEORGE *throws his manuscript down furiously.*)

(*Off.*) Murder – Rape – Wolves!

(GEORGE *opens his door and shouts at the enclosed bedroom
door.*)

GEORGE: Dorothy, I will not have my work interrupted by these
gratuitous acts of lupine delinquency!

(*The procession music, which had been allowed to fade out, is
brought up by the opening of the study door.*)

And turn that thing down! – you are deliberately feigning
an interest in brass band music to distract me from my
lecture!

(*He closes his door, and from behind it produces a quiver of
arrows and a bow. These he brings downstage and places them
on his desk. Pleasantly.*) Does, for the sake of argument,
God, so to speak, exist?

(*He returns upstage and finds an archery target, which he leans
up against the upstage bookcase, resting on the day-bed.*)

My method of inquiry this evening into certain aspects of
this hardy perennial may strike some of you as overly
engaging, but experience has taught me that to attempt to
sustain the attention of rival schools of academics by
argument alone is tantamount to constructing a Gothic arch
out of junket.

(*He extracts an arrow from the quiver.*)

Putting aside the God of Goodness, to whom we will return,
and taking first the God of Creation – or to give him his
chief philosophical *raison d'être*, the First Cause – we see
that a supernatural or divine origin is the logical
consequence of the assumption that one thing leads to
another, and that this series must have had a first term;
that, if you like, though chickens and eggs may alternate
back through the millennia, ultimately, we arrive at
something which, while perhaps no longer resembling
either a chicken or an egg, is nevertheless the first term of

that series and can itself only be attributed to a First Cause – or to give it its theological soubriquet, God. How well founded is such an assumption? Could it be, for instance, that chickens and eggs have been succeeding each other in one form or another literally for ever? My old friend – Mathematicians are quick to point out that they are familiar with many series which have no first term – such as the series of proper fractions between nought and one. What, they ask is the first, that is the smallest, of these fractions? A billionth? A trillionth? Obviously not: Cantor's proof that there is no greatest number ensures that there is no smallest fraction. There is no beginning. (*With a certain relish he notches his arrow into the bowstring*.) But it was precisely this notion of infinite series which in the sixth century BC led the Greek philosopher Zeno to conclude that since an arrow shot towards a target first had to cover half the distance, and then half the remainder, and then half the remainder after that, and so on *ad infinitum*, the result was, as I will now demonstrate, that though an arrow is always approaching its target, it never quite gets there, and Saint Sebastian died of fright.

(*He is about to fire the arrow, but changes his mind*.) Furthermore, by a similar argument he showed that *before* reaching the half-way point, the arrow had to reach the quarter-mark, and before that the eighth, and before that the sixteenth, and so on, with the result, remembering Cantor's proof, that the arrow *could not move at all*!

DOTTY: (*Off*) *Fire!*

(GEORGE *fires, startled before he was ready, and the arrow disappears into the top of the wardrobe*.)

Help – rescue – fire!

GEORGE: (*Shouts furiously*) Will you stop this childish nonsense! Thanks to you I have lost the element of surprise!

(*He tosses the bow away, tries to peer on tiptoe over the wardrobe, which is too high, and desists. He picks up his script, and then puts it down again, and sits on the corner of his desk, one leg swinging, arms folded. He notices that his socks do not*

match. The SECRETARY, *unruffled, waits patiently, her pencil poised. (It may as well be stated now that she never speaks.) Subdued at first.)* Look. . . . Consider my left sock. My left sock exists but it need not have done so. It is, we say, not necessary, but contingent. Why does my sock exist? Because a sock-maker made it, in one sense; because, in another, at some point previously, the conception of a sock arrived in the human brain; to keep my foot warm in a third, to make a profit in a fourth. There is reason and there is cause and there is the question, who made the sock-maker's maker? etcetera, very well, next! see, see, I move my foot which moves my sock. (*Walks.*) I and my foot and my sock all move round the room, which moves round the sun, which also moves, as Aristotle said, though not round the earth, he was wrong about that. There is reason and there is cause and there is motion, each in infinite regress towards a moment of origin and a point of ultimate reference – and one day! – as we stare into the fire at the mouth of our cave, suddenly! in an instant of grateful terror, we get it! – the one and only, sufficient unto himself, outside the action, uniquely immobile! – the Necessary Being, the First Cause, the Unmoved Mover!!
(*He collects himself.*)
Of the five proofs of God's existence put forward by St Thomas Aquinas, three depended on the simple idea that if an apparently endless line of dominoes is knocking itself over one by one then somewhere there is a domino which was *nudged*. And as regards dominoes, I haven't got any further than St Thomas. Everything has to begin somewhere and there is no answer to *that*. Except, of course, why does it? Why, since we accept the notion of infinity without end, should we not accept the logically identical notion of infinity without beginning? My old—Consider the series of proper fractions. Etcetera. (*To* SECRETARY) Then Cantor, then no beginning, etcetera, then Zeno. Insert: But the fact is, the first term of the series is not an infinite fraction but *zero*. It exists. God, so to speak, is nought. No, that can't be right. Continue. By

missing the point of a converging series Zeno overlooked the fallacy which is exemplified at its most picturesque in his famous paradoxes, which showed in every way but experience that an arrow could never reach its target, and that a tortoise given a head start in a race with, say, a hare, could never be overtaken – and by way of regaining your attention I will now demonstrate the nature of that fallacy; to which end I have brought with me a specially trained tortoise – (*which he takes from the smaller wooden box*) – and a similarly trained, damn and blast! – (*He has opened the larger box and found it empty. He looks round.*)

Thumper! Thumper, where are you, boy?

(*Failing to find Thumper under the desks or the bed, he leaves the room and, carrying the tortoise, enters the bedroom, opening the door wide and leaving it open as the bedroom lights up. Procession on screen. Procession music loud now, as though we travelled with him. The body of the* JUMPER *is nowhere in sight. However,* DOTTY's *nude body is sprawled face down, and apparently lifeless on the bed.* GEORGE *takes in the room at a glance, ignores* DOTTY, *and still calling for Thumper goes to look in the bathroom.*

GEORGE *reappears from the bathroom after a second or two. Mixed in with the TV music now is a snatch of commentary.*)

TV VOICE: . . . beautiful blue sky for the fly-past, and here they come!

(*Very loud: the jet planes scream and thunder on the sound track and scream and thunder across the screen. In mid-flight they are cut off –* GEORGE *has turned off the TV: silence and white screen.*)

GEORGE: Are you a proverb?

DOTTY: No, I'm a book.

GEORGE: *The Naked and the Dead.*

DOTTY: Stay with me!

(*The four lines have been rapid.* GEORGE *is now at the door, ready to leave.* DOTTY *has sat up on the bed.*)

Play with me . . .

GEORGE: (*Hesitating*) Now. . . ?

DOTTY: I mean *games* –

21

(GEORGE *makes to leave.*)

Be nice. (GEORGE *moves. Desperate.*) I'll let you!

(GEORGE *leaves, shutting the door and thus revealing the corpse to the audience. He re-enters, and the corpse is obscured again.*)*

GEORGE: Do I say 'My friend the late Bertrand Russell' or 'My late friend Bertrand Russell'? They both sound funny. (*Pause.*)

DOTTY: Probably because he wasn't your friend.

GEORGE: Well, I don't know about that.

DOTTY: (*Angrily*) He was *my* friend. If he hadn't asked me who was that bloke always hanging about, you'd never have met him.

GEORGE: Nevertheless, I did meet him, and we talked animatedly for some time.

DOTTY: As I recall, *you* talked animatedly for some time about language being the aniseed trail that draws the hounds of heaven when the metaphysical fox has gone to earth; he must have thought you were barmy.

GEORGE: (*Hurt*) I resent that. My metaphor of the fox and the hounds was an allusion, as Russell well understood, to his Theory of Descriptions.

DOTTY: Your metaphor of the fox and hounds with Bertie as the League Against Cruel Sports and yourself as John Peel was altogether lost on the poor man. He was far too busy trying to telephone Mao Tse Tung.

GEORGE: I was simply trying to bring his mind back to matters of universal import, and away from the day-to-day parochialism of international politics.

DOTTY: *Universal import!* You're living in dreamland!

GEORGE: Oh really? Well, I wouldn't have thought that trying to get the local exchange to put you through to Chairman Mao with the wine-waiter from the Pagoda Garden hanging

---

*In the event, the corpse was not hung on the back of the bedroom door, in the original production, but on the inside of the door of a cupboard adjacent to the bedroom door; the closing of the bedroom door mysteriously caused the opening of the cupboard door, a device gratefully borrowed from the famous Robert Dhery sketch in *La Plume de ma Tante*.

on to the bedroom extension to interpret, showed a grasp of the real world. (*He goes to leave.*) Thumper! Where are you, Thumper?

DOTTY: Georgie! – I'll let you.

(*He halts.*)

GEORGE: I don't want to be 'let'. Can't you see that it's an insult?

(DOTTY *drops back on to the bed in a real despair, and perhaps a real contrition.*)

DOTTY: Oh God . . . if only Archie would come.

GEORGE: (*Coldly*) Is he coming *again*?

DOTTY: I don't know. Do you mind?

GEORGE: Well, he's dropped in to see you every day this week. What am I supposed to think?

DOTTY: I don't believe I like your tone.

GEORGE: I have no tone. But I would like tonelessly to make the point that if he intends to visit you on a regular basis then either he should come after lunch or you should get up before it. Receiving in the bedroom is liable to get a woman talked about, unless it is an authentic salon.

DOTTY: How dare you? – Go on, get out and write your stupid speech for your dreamland debating society! I thought for once – I mean I seriously thought I might get a little – understanding – yes, finding myself in a bit of a spot, I seriously considered trusting you – for a little panache, without a lot of pedantic questions and hadn't-we-better-inform-the-authorities, I mean we should be able to rise *above* that – but not *you*, oh no, do you wonder I turn to Archie – ?

(*She lies down on the bed and pulls the cover over her.*)

GEORGE: (*Reckless, committed*) I can put two and two together, you know. Putting two and two together is my *subject*. I do not leap to hasty conclusions. I do not deal in suspicion and wild surmise. I examine the data; I look for logical inferences. We have on the one hand, that is to say in bed, an attractive married woman whose relationship with her husband stops short only of the issue of a ration book; we have on the other hand daily visits by a celebrated ladies' man who rings the doorbell, is admitted by Mrs Thing who shows him into the bedroom, whence he emerges an hour later looking more than a little complacent and crying, 'Don't worry, I'll let myself out!'

(*He lapses into a calm suavity.*)

Now let us see. What can we make of it all? Wife in bed, daily visits by gentleman caller. Does anything suggest itself?

DOTTY: (*Calmly*) Sounds to me he's the doctor.

(GEORGE *is staggered.*)

GEORGE: (*Pause*) Doctor? . . . The Vice-Chancellor?

DOTTY: (*Spiritedly*) You *know* he's a bloody doctor!

GEORGE: I know he's a qualified psychiatrist, but he doesn't practise. I mean he isn't a chap who goes around looking down people's *throats*. His line is psychotics . . . manic depressives – schizos – fantasisers –

(DOTTY *picks up her mirror and starts brushing her hair. Catching up.*) You mean you're bad again? (*Pause.*) I'm sorry. . . . How was I supposed to know you were . . .

DOTTY: I'm all right in here.

(*Pause.*)

GEORGE: Why did he bring you flowers? Not that there's any reason, of course, why he shouldn't bring you flowers.

DOTTY: Quite.

GEORGE: I mean, he's our friend, more or less. He likes you. Do you like him?

DOTTY: He's all right in his way.

GEORGE: What way is that?

DOTTY: Oh, you know.

GEORGE: No. What does he do?

DOTTY: He's a doctor.

(*Pause.*)

He keeps my spirits up.

GEORGE: Does he? That's . . . good.

DOTTY: I won't see him any more, if you like. (*Turns to him.*) I'll see you. If you like.

(GEORGE *examines the new tone, and decides the moment is genuine.*)

GEORGE: (*Softening*) Oh, Dotty. . . . The first day you walked
into my class . . . I thought, '*That's* better!' . . . It was a
wet day . . . your hair was wet . . . and I thought, 'The
hyacinth girl' . . . and 'How my hair is growing thin'.

DOTTY: And I thought, 'I'll sit quiet and they won't find out
I'm stupid' . . . and 'What a modest way with lovely
words', and 'How his hair is growing thin'.

GEORGE: And you started to sit nearer the front.

DOTTY: You didn't look any younger.

GEORGE: (*Pang*) And then you fell among theatricals.

DOTTY: But it was still all right.

GEORGE: Oh yes, for a time. And then again, it wasn't. And
then again, it sometimes is, even now, when all else fails
you.

DOTTY: (*Going to him*) George, I'm in a bit of a spot.

GEORGE: What?

DOTTY: (*Touching him*) Promise not to be stuffy.

GEORGE: Stuffy? Me? Tell me everything. In a minute.

DOTTY: You haven't shaved.

GEORGE: I'll shave then. In a minute. What sort of spot?
(*He embraces her.*)

DOTTY: Actually I feel a bit starved.

GEORGE: So do I.

DOTTY: Food I meant.

GEORGE: Afterwards.

DOTTY: (*Disengaging herself*) Before.

GEORGE: On second thoughts.
(*He is leaving again.*)

DOTTY: Haven't you invented God yet?

GEORGE: Nearly, I'm having him typed out.

DOTTY: Please stay.

GEORGE: Really?

DOTTY: Really.

GEORGE: I'll shave then.
(*Loud jets fly overhead.*)
What's going on?

DOTTY: It's the fly-past.

GEORGE: Oh yes . . . the Radical Liberals . . . It seems in

25

dubious taste. Soldiers, fighter planes . . . After all, it was a general election not a *coup d'état*.

DOTTY: It's funny you should say that.

GEORGE: Why?

DOTTY: Archie says it was a *coup d'état* not a general election.

GEORGE: Glib nonsense. You can't get away with that sort of thing. The skeletons in the cupboard will all come out in the wash.

DOTTY: Then God help me.

GEORGE: Furthermore I had a vote.

DOTTY: It's not the voting that's democracy, it's the counting.

GEORGE: I don't believe you know anything about it. You are the wife of an academic. That means you are twice removed from the centre of events.
(He pauses on his way to the bathroom.)
What did you mean, God help you?

DOTTY: I didn't mean to bring him into it. It just slipped out.
(He disappears back into the bathroom.)
(Still merry) And yet, Professor, one can't help wondering at the persistence of the reflex, the universal constant unthinking appeal to the non-existent God who is presumed dead. Perhaps he's only missing in action, shot down behind the thin yellow lines of advancing Rad-Libs and getting himself together to go BOO!
(He returns holding his razor.)

GEORGE: Have you been shaving your legs?

DOTTY: And so our tutorials descended, from the metaphysical to the merely physical . . . not so much down to earth as down to the carpet, do you remember?
(New tone. GEORGE, half-foamed, bibbed, sits on the bed.)
That was the year of 'The Concept of Knowledge', your masterpiece, and the last decent title left after Ryle bagged 'The Concept of Mind' and Archie bagged 'The Problem of Mind' and Ayer bagged 'The Problem of Knowledge' – and 'The Concept of Knowledge' might have made you if you had written it, but we were still on the carpet when an American with an Italian name working in Melbourne bagged it for a rather bad book which sold four copies in

London, three to unknown purchasers and the fourth to
yourself. He'd stolen a march while you were still comparing
knowledge in the sense of having-experience-of, with knowledge
in the sense of being-acquainted-with, and knowledge in the
sense of inferring facts with knowledge in the sense of
comprehending truths, and all the time as you got more and
more acquainted with, though no more comprehending of,
the symbolic patterns on my Persian carpet, it was knowing in
the biblical sense of screwing that you were learning about and
maybe there's a book in you yet —

GEORGE: (*Leaving*) Philosophy calls.

DOTTY: George, you can't go . . . there's a corpse in the
cupboard.

GEORGE: Whenever you're like this I always think how unjust it
is that so many people must have looked at us and said,
What on earth made *her* marry *him*? (*To the goldfish*) Good
morning. His water needs changing. What were you going
to tell me?

DOTTY: It doesn't matter.

GEORGE: You said you had a problem.

DOTTY: I think it needs a radical liberal solution. You wouldn't
be sympathetic.

(*She takes the goldfish bowl into the bathroom.*)

GEORGE: (*Carefully reassuring himself*) Oh I don't know.
Radicalism has a fine and honourable tradition in this country.
It will always involve a healthy scepticism about inherited
means and ends, that is all.

(DOTTY *re-enters with the goldfish bowl, emptied and upside
down, over her head. She walks with the gait of a moonwalker.*
GEORGE *ignores her.*)

I mean, it would be presumptuous to condemn radical ideas
simply because they appear to me to be self-evidently stupid
and criminal if they do happen to be at the same time
radical. (DOTTY, *moonwalking, affects to find and stoop for a
small coin, which she holds up for* GEORGE, *who does not
pause.*) 'The Moon and Sixpence'.

It is, after all, a radical idea to ensure freedom of the
individual by denying it to groups.

27

(DOTTY *takes off the fish bowl and replaces it on its table, somewhat pointlessly now.*)

 Indeed, any party which calls itself radical might be said to have forfeited this claim if it *neglected* to take over the broadcasting services and send the Church Commissioners to prison –

DOTTY: It wasn't the Church Commissioners, it was property companies and Masters of Foxhounds.

GEORGE: I thought the Church Commissioners *were* a property company.

DOTTY: They were dispossessed.

 (*She tosses him a* Times *newspaper from the table beside the bed.*)

GEORGE: Well, what about the Church Commissioners who were also Masters of Foxhounds?

DOTTY: *I* don't know – Darling, I'm starving –

GEORGE: (*Raving*) And how is the Church to pay its clergy? Are they going to pull down the churches?

DOTTY: Yes. (*He gapes.*) The Church is going to be rationalized.

GEORGE: *Rationalized?* (*Furiously*) You can't rationalize the Thirty-Nine Articles!

DOTTY: No, no . . . not the faith, the fabric. You remember how they rationalized the railways? – well, now they're going to rationalize the Church. (*Pause.*) There was an announcement in *The Times*.

GEORGE: Who by?

DOTTY: The Archbishop of Canterbury. Clegthorpe.

GEORGE: *Clegthorpe? Sam Clegthorpe?*

DOTTY: It's been made a political appointment, like judges.

GEORGE: Are you telling me that the Radical Liberal spokesman for Agriculture has been made Archbishop of Canterbury?!!

DOTTY: Don't shout at *me* . . . I suppose if you think of him as a sort of . . . shepherd, ministering to his flock . . .

GEORGE: But he's an *agnostic*.

DOTTY: (*Capitulating*) I absolutely agree with you – *nobody* is going to have any confidence in him. It's like the Chairman of the Electricity Board believing in gas.

GEORGE: (*Shouts*) No, it is not! (*An exhausted pause.*) You're making it up. You just like to get me going.

DOTTY: Do you find it incredible that a man with a scientific background should be Archbishop of Canterbury?

GEORGE: How the hell do *I* know what I find incredible? Credibility is an expanding field. . . . Sheer disbelief hardly registers on the face before the head is nodding with all the wisdom of instant hindsight. 'Archbishop Clegthorpe? Of course! The inevitable capstone to a career in veterinary medicine!' What happened to the old Archbishop?

DOTTY: He abdicated . . . or resigned or uncoped himself –

GEORGE: (*Thoughtfully*) Dis-mantled himself, perhaps.

(DOTTY *turns on the TV: the Moon.*)

Good God! (*At window*) I can actually *see* Clegthorpe! – marching along, attended by two chaplains in belted raincoats.

DOTTY: Is he wearing a mitre?

GEORGE: Yes. He's blessing people to right and left. He must be drunk.

(*He stares out of the window.* DOTTY *stares at the TV.*)

DOTTY: Poor moon man, falling home like Lucifer. (*She turns off the TV: Screen goes white.*) . . . Of course, to somebody *on* it, the moon is always full, so the local idea of a sane action may well differ from ours. (*Pause; stonily.*) When they first landed, it was as though I'd seen a unicorn on the television news . . . Very interesting, of course. But it certainly spoils unicorns. (*Pause.*) I tried to explain it to the analyst when everybody in sight was asking me what was the matter . . . 'What's the matter, darling?' . . . 'What *happened*, baby?' What could I say? I came over funny at work so I went home early. It must happen often enough to a working girl. And why must the damned show go on anyway? So it stopped right then and there, and in a way my retirement was the greatest triumph of my career. Because nobody left.

GEORGE: (*To himself*) Sam Clegthorpe!

DOTTY: For nearly an hour they all sat out front, staring at that stupid spangled moon, and they weren't waiting for their money's worth, they were waiting for *news. Is she all right?* . . . Oh yes, not bad for a bored housewife, eh? – not at all

29

bad for a one-time student amateur bored with keeping house for her professor. And they're still waiting! – my retirement is now almost as long as my career, but they're waiting for me to come back out, and finish my song. And writing me love letters in the mean time. That's right, *not* so bloody bad for a second-class honours with a half-good voice and a certain variety of shakes. It's no good, though. They thought it was overwork or alcohol, but it was just those little grey men in goldfish bowls, clumping about in their lead boots on the television news; it was very interesting, but it certainly spoiled that Juney old moon; and much else besides . . . The analyst went barking up the wrong tree, of course; I should never have mentioned unicorns to a Freudian.

(GEORGE *turns back from the view.*)

GEORGE: (*Serenely*) Archbishop Clegthorpe! That must be the high point of scientism; from here on the Darwinian revolution declines to its own origins. Man has gone ape and God is in the ascendant, and it will end as it began, with him gazing speculatively down on the unpeopled earth as the moon rises over the smoking landscape of vulcanite cliffs and lakes of clinker.

DOTTY: Do you think it is . . . *significant* that it's impossible to imagine anyone building a church on the moon?

GEORGE: If God exists, he certainly existed before religion. He is a philosopher's God, logically inferred from self-evident premises. That he should have been taken up by a glorified supporters' club is only a matter of psychological interest.

DOTTY: Archie says the Church is a monument to irrationality.

(*He turns and shouts at her with surprising anger.*)

GEORGE: The National Gallery is a monument to irrationality! Every concert hall is a monument to irrationality! – and so is a nicely kept garden, or a lover's favour, or a home for stray dogs! You stupid woman, if rationality were the criterion for things being allowed to exist, the world would be one gigantic field of soya beans!

(*He picks up his tortoise and balances it lovingly on the palm of his hand, at the level of his mouth. Apologetically.*) Wouldn't it, Pat?

The irrational, the emotional, the whimsical . . . these are the stamp of humanity which makes reason a civilizing force. In a wholly rational society the moralist will be a variety of crank, haranguing the bus queue with the demented certitude of one blessed with privileged information 'Good and evil are metaphysical absolutes!' What did I come in for? (*Looking round.*)

DOTTY: All this talk about beans reminds me . . . I left something for Mrs Doings to put in the oven – Could you – ?

GEORGE: No, I couldn't. You know where the kitchen is –

DOTTY: Where?

GEORGE: Where's Mrs Thingummy?

DOTTY: It's a national holiday. I expect she's down there somewhere, waving a little yellow flag.

GEORGE: Oh yes – *she* would be in on it. In fact I can't think of anyone more susceptible to the Rad-Lib philosophy: 'No problem is insoluble given a big enough plastic bag.' (*He's leaving.*)

DOTTY: You don't happen to *have* a large plastic bag, do you?

GEORGE: Can you remember what I came in for?

DOTTY: *Please don't leave me!* I don't want to be left, to cope . . .

GEORGE: Dotty, I'm sorry, I must . . . I'm sorry if it's one of your bad days, but things will get better.

DOTTY: There's no question of things getting better. Things are one way or they are another way; 'better' is how we see them, Archie says, and I don't personally, very much; though sometimes he makes them seem not so bad after all – no, that's wrong, too: he knows not 'seems'. Things do not *seem*, on the one hand, they *are*; and on the other hand, bad is not what they can *be*. They can be green, or square, or Japanese, loud, fatal, waterproof or vanilla-flavoured; and the same for actions, which can be *disapproved of*, or comical, unexpected, saddening or good television, variously, depending on who frowns, laughs, jumps, weeps or wouldn't have missed it for the world. Things and actions, you understand, can have any number of real and verifiable properties. But good and bad, better and worse, these are not real properties of things, they are just expressions of our feelings about them.

GEORGE: Archie says.

DOTTY: (*Pause*) Unfortunately, I don't feel so good today. If you like, I won't see him. It'll be just you and me under that old-fashioned, silvery harvest moon, occasionally blue, jumped over by cows and coupleted by Junes, invariably shining on the one I love; well-known in Carolina, much loved in Allegheny, familiar in Vermont; (*The screw turning in her*) *Keats's* bloody moon! – for what has made the sage or poet write but the fair paradise of nature's light – And *Milton's* bloody moon! rising in clouded majesty, at length apparent queen – And Shelley's sodding maiden, with white fire laden, whom mortals call the – (*Weeping*) *Oh yes, things were in place then!*

(*She weeps on George's uncomprehending heart. He strokes her hair. She speaks into his chest.*)

Oh, Georgie. . . .

(*He strokes her hair. He doesn't really know what to do. So he plays with her hair for what seems a long time, lifting up her hair, running it through his fingers, looking at it, separating strands of hair. His mind grapples with hair, and then drifts, and stops.*)

GEORGE: Have you seen Thumper?

(*He is immediately ashamed of himself. But he has killed it. They separate.* DOTTY *straightens up.* GEORGE *walks to the door, taking his tortoise.*)

Did Bertrand Russell ever . . . mention me, after that?

DOTTY: Frequently. He used to sing (*Sings.*) D'ye ken George Moore with his coat so gay, d'ye ken George Moore, D. Phil. M.A. D'ye ken George Moore when he's far, far away . . .

(*There is nothing to do but go, so he goes. Into the study. He has closed the bedroom door. The* JUMPER *hangs on the door.* DOTTY *regards the corpse without expression. During the next scene in the study, the light remains in the bedroom.* DOTTY, *during the scene, lifts the corpse off its hook and sits it in an upstage chair.*

GEORGE *enters the study. His face is still foamed.*

The SECRETARY *has been typing out his dictation.*
She hands him the sheets.
*The merest trace of interest in the fact that he has shaving foam
on his face.*)

GEORGE: I take it then that we are all agreed that God exists,
cries of, 'Oh!', I mean a First Cause, cries of, 'Oh, Oh!',
you have not been giving me your proper attention, I will
attempt a resumé, uproar, cries of 'Resign' – Firstly, is
God? Secondly that every series has a first term is a
condition that makes God a logical necessity. Thirdly, every
series does, the notion of infinity without beginning being
rejected *a priori*, thank you. (*Snatches page off desk.*)
Fifthly, mathematics is not simply the technique of
counting –
(*Breaks off. Takes new sheet of paper.*)
To which end I have brought with me a specially trained
tortoise –
(*Breaks off again.*) Pat!?
(*He heads back towards the bedroom where* DOTTY *has just
dumped the* JUMPER *into the chair. The chair is upstage facing
the audience.* DOTTY *is standing up against the chair with her
back to the audience. The tortoise has been left downstage right,
so* GEORGE *is going to cross the bedroom behind Dotty's back.
The Jumper's yellow trousers are ill concealed by Dotty's body.*
GEORGE *enters.*
As GEORGE *opens the door,* DOTTY *calmly lets her robe slip
down her back until it hangs like a drape below her buttocks,
her arms, still in the sleeves, held out to the sides; thus
concealing the* JUMPER *from view. Thus, she is naked from the
thighs up, back view.* GEORGE *glances casually at her as he
crosses the room.*)

GEORGE: *Bottom?*
(DOTTY *lifts the robe to cover her bottom.*)
Back. . . . Somebody's back. . . ?
(*He picks up the tortoise.* DOTTY *turns to look at him
coquettishly over her shoulder. He is recrossing the room towards
the door.*)
Lulu's back! – in town – Very good!

(*He leaves, closing the door, and re-enters the study.*
DOTTY *pulls her robe on again.*
The bedroom fades out.
In the study, he picks up the bow and an arrow.
The doorbell rings. He hesitates.)
(*To himself*) The Vice-Chancellor?
He's early. (*Looks at his watch.*) Good God, it's
unprofessional conduct. He's only just *left.* (*The door bell*
rings again. He marches to the door, brandishing his bow and
arrow, and, putting his mouth to the tortoise's ear, or
thereabouts, confides in it.)
Now might I do it, Pat.
(*He opens the front door.*
It is INSPECTOR BONES. *He carries a bunch of flowers.*
The door is opened to him by a man holding a bow and
arrow in one hand and a tortoise in the other, his face covered
in shaving foam. BONES *recoils from the spectacle, and*
GEORGE *is somewhat taken aback too. A rapid exchange*
follows . . .)
BONES: Ah! – Bones!
GEORGE: What?
BONES: As in rags-and.
GEORGE: Rags and bones???
BONES: Yes – no. Bones' the name, as in dem bones, dem bones
. . . (*Pause.*) . . . dem dry bones. That's a tortoise, is it?
GEORGE: I'm sorry, I was expecting a psychiatrist.
BONES: No really?
(BONES *is himself again, master of any situation. He advances*
past GEORGE.)
GEORGE: I'm really rather busy.
(BONES *looks at* GEORGE *with unconcealed interest.*)
BONES: What is it that you do?
GEORGE: I'm a professor of moral philosophy.
BONES: (*Wagging a finger*) I'm very glad you said that, son.
(BONES *continues his inspection of the hall.*)
GEORGE: Perhaps I can help you.
BONES: In my inquiries, you mean, or just generally? Think
carefully before you answer – if it gets about that you're

helping me in my *inquiries*, bang goes your credit at the off-licence for a start. Inspector Bones, CID – tell Miss Moore I'm here, there's a good lad.

GEORGE: (*Rather coldly*) It's *Mrs* Moore, actually.

BONES: Moore is her married name?

GEORGE: Yes, Moore is *my* name.

BONES: (*Shrewdly*) You are the husband.

GEORGE: Yes.

BONES: Professor . . . Moore.

GEORGE: Yes. . . . (*Lightening*.) Yes, I'm something of a logician *myself*.

BONES: Really? Sawing ladies in half, that sort of thing?

GEORGE: *L*ogician.

(BONES *is casing the hall expertly, just with his eyes*.)
Would you like me to take your flowers, Inspector?

BONES: I was hoping to see Miss Moore personally.

GEORGE: Well, it's awfully nice of you to come round. . . .

BONES: Not at all. If I'm going to arrest her, I can hardly do it by Interflora.

GEORGE: Arrest her?

BONES: Do not be misled by appearances, Charlie. Miss Moore is a great favourite in the Force and I have knocked down many a man who has defaced her photograph in the station canteen – *but*, the law is implacable, it makes no distinction between rich and poor, famous and anonymous, innocent and— I mean, Jack, if the telephone call which set in motion this inquiry was the whim of a lunatic, as I myself suspect, then I will simply take the opportunity of presenting this token tribute to a fine actress, a great singer and a true lady – after which, I will take my leave, perhaps with her autograph on the cover of this much played much loved gramophone record – (*from a capacious inside-pocket of his raincoat*) – and, who knows? the lingering touch of a kiss brushed against an admirer's cheek . . . (*Reverie* . . .)
BUT!– if it so happens that there is any truth in the allegations concerning events in this luxury penthouse yesterday night, then there are going to be some bruised petals underfoot as the full majesty of the law comes down

on her like a ton of bricks, you take my meaning, Ferdinand?
(*Entering the study.*) Is this the scene of your morals?
(*The* SECRETARY *stares at him.*)
(*Unnecessarily.*) Don't move.
(BONES *acts as if he owns the place, picking things up and putting them down; glancing over the typewritten sheets on George's desk.*)

GEORGE: This is my secretary – she and I were just –
(*He puts down the tortoise and the archery kit, and wipes his face hastily.*)
Oh – I should explain –

BONES: I prefer to use my imagination. When will your wife be back?

GEORGE: She's in bed – indisposed – waiting for the doctor.

BONES: Lockjaw?

GEORGE: No.

BONES: Then we can have a chat. Is God what?
(*He is reading the first page of the typescript.*)

GEORGE: What? – Oh – it's a paper I am presenting to the symposium tonight at the university. I am one of two main speakers on the subject, 'Man – good, bad or indifferent?' The subject is in fact the same every year but there is enough disagreement about its meaning to ensure a regular change of topic. It is the first time I have been asked to speak, you know . . . I had hoped to set British moral philosophy back forty years, which is roughly when it went off the rails, but unfortunately though my convictions are intact and my ideas coherent, I can't seem to find the words . . .

BONES: Well, 'Are God?' is wrong for a start.

GEORGE: Or rather, the words betray the thoughts they are supposed to express. Even the most generalized truth begins to look like special pleading as soon as you trap it in language. It would be a great opportunity if only I could seize it . . . I mean, it's really the event of the year. (*Pause.*) In the world of moral philosophy, that is.

BONES: (*Putting down the script*) It's not a world I move in very much.

GEORGE: No.

BONES: Show business is my main interest, closely followed by crime detection. If this is the largest room in the flat I don't think I'll be troubling you long.

GEORGE: Oh. Well . . . the bedroom is about the same size, but of course there's the main living room. . . .

BONES: Living room? Big room?

GEORGE: It is big, yes, it was the ballroom before the place was converted into flats.

BONES: High ceiling?

GEORGE: Yes.

BONES: Ah. Take a troupe of acrobats, would it?

GEORGE: (*Pause*) Yes. I'm afraid so.

BONES: Getting my drift, Sidney? Let's have a look.

(BONES *walks out of the study. After a moment of nonplussed hesitance,* GEORGE *follows quickly, catching up outside the study door, which he closes behind him.*)

GEORGE: Inspector! – I think I can help you in your inquiries. I'm your man. I am the mystery telephone caller.

BONES: (*Pause*) You laid information against your wife, sir?

GEORGE: Yes. Well, it was really against myself more than my wife.

BONES: Anonymously. Against yourself?

GEORGE: Yes.

BONES: You have a funny way of going about things.

GEORGE: I don't understand you. I didn't give my name because I could hardly register a complaint about the noise issuing from my own flat. So I pretended to be a neighbour who couldn't sleep.

BONES: Your phone call was about the noise?

GEORGE: Yes.

BONES: You didn't mention – an acrobat?

GEORGE: Did I?

BONES: Or a naked woman swinging from the chandeliers?

GEORGE: Oh yes! I'm ashamed to say I did. I said I saw her from the window opposite. I thought a suggestion of immorality might get the police round more quickly than mere exuberance. Not a word of truth in it, of course. I mean about me being at a window opposite. And I

37

withdraw the complaint anyway; the young woman is of excellent character and notably self-composed as a rule. It was a side of her I'd never seen before. High spirits, no doubt. Incidentally, I don't know who answers the phone at your place but he told me to draw my curtains and remember that I was young once; not what one expects.

BONES: (*He produces a notebook*) Who was at this party. . . ?

GEORGE: Oh . . . academics, writers, doctors, philosophers, actors, musicians, party-workers, acrobats; and of course the Vice-Chancellor who is a bit of everything.

BONES: A mixed bunch.

GEORGE: Not really. I mean, they're all local Rad-Lib celebrities. It was a victory party.

BONES: You were not celebrating it yourself?

GEORGE: No, I'm not interested in politics. I was trying to write my paper. Apart from bunking down on the couch for a couple of hours at dawn, I've been hard at it. Oh, I popped in once or twice, mainly to tell them to keep the music down. My paper was not coming well and I anticipated a strongly argued riposte from Professor McFee, who obviously thought he had the matter well in hand since he was one of the people actually making all the noise.

BONES: Professor McFee?

GEORGE: Professor of Logic, and my chief adversary at the symposium tonight. A very good man in his way, though perhaps I should describe him as generally approved of – he doesn't, of course, believe in good and bad as such.

BONES: Really? How do you mean?

GEORGE: He thinks good and bad aren't actually *good* and *bad* in any absolute or metaphysical sense, he believes them to be categories of our own making, social and psychological conventions which we have evolved in order to make living in groups a practical possibility, in much the same way as we have evolved the rules of tennis without which Wimbledon Fortnight would be a complete shambles, do you see? For example, McFee would hold that when we speak of, say, telling the truth as being 'good', and, er, casual murder as being 'bad', you don't really want to go into all this, do you?

BONES: (*His pencil poised, his eyes wide*) I am enthralled.

GEORGE: Oh. Well, in simple terms he believes that on the whole people should tell the truth all right, and keep their promises, and so on – but on the sole grounds that if everybody went around telling lies and breaking their word as a matter of course, normal life would be impossible. Of course, he is defining normality in terms of the truth being told and promises being kept, etcetera, so the definition is circular and not worth very much, but the point is it allows him to conclude that telling lies is not *sinful* but simply anti-social.

BONES: And murder?

GEORGE: And murder, too, yes.

BONES: He thinks there's nothing *wrong* with killing people?

GEORGE: Well, put like that, of course . . . But *philosophically*, he doesn't think it's actually, inherently wrong in itself, no.

BONES: (*Amazed*) What sort of philosophy is that?

GEORGE: Mainstream, I'd call it. Orthodox mainstream.

(BONES *scratches his head.* GEORGE *gazes at him innocently.*)

BONES: How would you describe him – this McFee?

GEORGE: Duncan? Well, he's completely mad, of course. They all are . . . Well, Inspector, I'm sorry to have wasted your time, but I don't think there's any need to trouble you further. An Englishman's home is his castle, eh?

(*He opens the front door.* BONES *ignores it.*)

BONES: (*With irony*) In these cases, we *do* like to have a look at the scene of the crime –

GEORGE: Oh, really? What for?

BONES: It's traditional . . . About mad McFee – has he got a gun?

GEORGE: I don't know. I believe he has a fishing-rod – Oh *no*, you don't understand. He wouldn't *kill* anyone. He's against it. He thinks it shouldn't be allowed. He would prefer it to be kept to a minimum. Otherwise – shambles. He's no more capable of killing someone than the Archbishop of Canterbury. (*Small pause.*) Not *as* capable.

BONES: Well, if that's the case, I don't see any difference whether he thinks he's obeying the Ten Commandments or the rules of tennis.

GEORGE: The difference is, the rules of tennis can be changed.

BONES: Where can I find a vase?

GEORGE: A vase? In the kitchen.

> (*Immediately: Procession music.*
> *Procession on screen.*
> *Light up bedroom.*
> BONES *exits to kitchen.* GEORGE *closes the front door.*
> DOTTY *hears the door.*)

DOTTY: Archie! . . .

> (DOTTY *has been watching the TV screen. The* JUMPER *is hidden.* GEORGE *goes to the bedroom door, and opens it.*)

GEORGE: (*From the doorway*) It's not Archie, it's the police.

> (DOTTY *turns off the TV. The screen goes white.*)

DOTTY: What?

GEORGE: Inspector Bones. It's about last night. Malicious complaints. Allegations.

DOTTY: What sort of allegations?

GEORGE: (*Embarrassed, playing it down*) Anonymous phone call, apparently. Tell you later.

> (*He tries to leave, the first of several false exits by him.* DOTTY *is numb.*)

DOTTY: Did he mention an acrobat?

GEORGE: Yes. Don't worry, I'll smooth him over.

DOTTY: *Smooth him over?*

GEORGE: He's gone to inspect the scene of the crime. What an absurd fuss.

DOTTY: George . . . you knew about it?

> (GEORGE *mistakes her gratitude for suspicion.*)

GEORGE: Look, I'm perfectly willing to take the blame.

DOTTY: Oh, George . . . George . . . will you?

> (*She kisses him.*)

GEORGE: If he's going to be bloody-minded, I'll shoot him in here.

DOTTY: *Georgie!*

GEORGE: You can try your charms on him. He's dead keen to meet you. (*False exit.*) He seems quite interested in philosophy.

DOTTY: Oh?

GEORGE: Yes. I think I can get through to him. Get him to see that one can easily get things out of proportion.

DOTTY: (*Enthusiastically*) That's just what Archie said about it.

GEORGE: (*Nods, false exit*) Said about what?

DOTTY: Well, about poor Duncan McFee.

GEORGE: What about Duncan McFee?

DOTTY: There's no need to get it out of proportion. It's a great pity, but it's not as though the alternative were immortality.

GEORGE: (*Nods; stops nodding*) Sorry?

BONES: (*Offstage*) Hello! (*Enters from kitchen.*)

(DOTTY *pushes* GEORGE *out of the bedroom and closes the door. The bedroom blacks out.* GEORGE *turns to meet* BONES *who has appeared and is coming upstage, his flowers now in a metal vase.*) Tell me something – Who *are* these acrobats?

GEORGE: Logical positivists, mainly, with a linguistic analyst or two, a couple of Benthamite Utilitarians . . . lapsed Kantians and empiricists generally . . . and of course the usual Behaviourists . . . a mixture of the more philosophical members of the university gymnastics team and the more gymnastic members of the Philosophy School. The close association between gymnastics and philosophy is I believe unique to this university and owes itself to the Vice-Chancellor, who is of course a first-rate gymnast, though an indifferent philosopher.

(BONES *stares at him and then walks into the study and sits down like a man who needs to sit down.* GEORGE *follows him.*) A curious combination of interests, but of course in ancient classical Greece –

BONES: We are not *in* ancient bloody classical Greece.

GEORGE: I absolutely agree with you. In fact, I will have nothing to do with it. And in spite of the Vice-Chancellor's insistence that I can jump better than I think, I have always maintained the converse to be the case . . . In the circumstances I was lucky to get the Chair of Moral Philosophy. (*His tone suggests, rightly, that this is not much of a prize.*) Only the Chair of Divinity lies further below the salt, and *that's* been vacant for six months since the last occupant pulled a ham string.

BONES: Then why didn't you . . . jump along with the rest?

GEORGE: I belong to a school which regards all sudden movements as ill-bred. On the other hand, McFee, who sees professorship as a licence for eccentricity, and whose chief delusion is that Edinburgh is the Athens of the North, very soon learned to jump a great deal better than he ever thought, and was rewarded with the Chair of Logic.

BONES: Are you telling me that the Professor of Logic is a part-time acrobat?

GEORGE: Yes. More of a gymnast, really – the acrobatics are just the social side.

BONES: I find this very hard to believe.

GEORGE: Oh, really? Why's that?

BONES: (*Rising*) I don't like it, Clarence! The way I had it, some raving nutter phones up the station with a lot of bizarre allegations starting off with a female person swinging naked from the chandeliers at Dorothy Moore's Mayfair residence and ending up with a professor picked off while doing handsprings for the cabaret, and as far as I'm concerned it's got fruit-cake written all over it; so I tell my Sergeant to have a cup of tea and off I go thinking to myself, at last a chance to pay my respects in person, and blow me if it doesn't start to look straight up as soon as I put one foot in the door – Don't go, will you?

(*He has moved to the door, with his vase of flowers, and leaves, closing the study door behind him. In front of the bedroom door, he briefly smooths his hair, brushes his lapels with his hands, brings out the gramophone record (which has a picture of* DOTTY *on it), and knocks on the bedroom door, a mere tap, and enters the bedroom.*

The light is romantic: pink curtains have been drawn across the french window, and there is a rosy hue to the lighting.

DOTTY, *gowned, coiffed, stunning, rises to face the Inspector. Music is heard . . . the trumpet-call from* Fidelio. DOTTY *and* BONES *face each other, frozen like lovers in a dream.* BONES *raises his head slightly, and the trumpets are succeeded by a loud animal bray, a mating call.* DOTTY, *her arms out towards him, breathes, 'Inspector . . .' like a verbal caress. From* BONES's *lifeless fingers, the vase drops. There is a noise such as would*

*have been made had he dropped it down a long flight of stone
stairs.*
BONES *is dumbstruck.*
DOTTY *lets go a long slow smile:* 'Inspector . . .'
From behind the closed curtains, the stiff dead JUMPER *falls
into the room like a too-hastily-leaned plank.*
Quick fade to blackout, in bedroom only.
*None of the sounds have been imaginary: they have come from
George's coincidental tape-recorder, which he now switches off
and rewinds slightly,* GEORGE *picks up his manuscript, snaps
his fingers at the* SECRETARY, *and starts off.*)
GEORGE: Professor McFee's introductory paper, which it is my
privilege to dispute, has I think been distributed to all of
you. In an impressive display of gymnastics, ho ho, thank
you, Professor McFee bends over backwards to
demonstrate that moral judgements belong to the same class
as aesthetic judgements; that the phrases 'good man' and
'good music' are prejudiced in exactly the same way; in
short, that goodness, whether in men or in music, depends
on your point of view. By discrediting the idea of beauty as
an aesthetic absolute, he hopes to discredit by association
the idea of goodness as a moral absolute and as a first step
he directs us to listen to different kinds of music. (*He
reaches for the tape-recorder.*) Professor McFee refers us in
particular to the idea of beauty as conceived by Beethoven
on the one hand, and here I am glad to be able to assist him
. . . (*Plays* Fidelio *again.*) . . . and, on the other hand, as
conceived by a group of musicians playing at a wedding
feast in a part of Equatorial Africa visited only by the
makers of television documentaries, one of which the
Professor happened to see on a rare occasion when he
wasn't out and about jumping through the Vice-
Chancellor's hoop, I can't say that, one of which he
happened to see. He invites us to agree with him that
beauty is a diverse notion and not a universal one.
Personally, I would have agreed to this without demur, but
the Professor, whose reading is as wide as his jumping is
high . . .

(*The* SECRETARY *raises her head.*)

. . . all right, all right, the Professor bolsters up his
argument with various literary references including a telling
extract from *Tarzan of the Apes* in which the boy Tarzan on
seeing his face for the first time reflected in a jungle pool,
bewails his human ugliness as compared to the beauty of
the apes, among whom he had grown up. I won't dwell on
Professor McFee's inability to distinguish between fact and
fiction, but as regards the musical references it might be
worth pointing out that the sounds made by Beethoven and
the Africans might have certain things in common which
are not shared by the sound of, say, a bucket of coal being
emptied on to a tin roof. Indeed, I have brought with me
tonight two further trumpet recordings, starting off with
the trumpeting of an elephant . . . (*He plays the braying
sound heard before.*) . . . and I invite Professor McFee to
admit that the difference between that and his beloved
Beethoven may owe more to some mysterious property of
the music than to his classically trained ear. Anticipating his
reply that the latter sound is more beautiful to an elephant,
I riposte with . . . (*He plays the remaining sound, as heard
before.*) . . . which is the sound made by a trumpet falling
down a flight of stone stairs. However, it is not my present
concern to dispute Professor McFee's view on aesthetics but
only to make clear what those views must lead him to, and
they lead him to the conclusion that if the three sets of
noises which we might label 'Beethoven', 'elephant' and
'stairs', were playing in an empty room where no one could
hear them, then it could not be said that within the room
any one set of noises was in any way superior to either of
the other two. Which may, of course, be the case, but
Professor McFee does not stay to consider such a *reductio ad
absurdum*, for he has bigger fish to fry, and so he goes on to
show, likewise but at even greater length, that the word
'good' has also meant different things to different people at
different times, an exercise which combines simplicity with
futility in a measure he does not apparently suspect, for on
the one hand it is not a statement which anyone would

44

dispute, and on the other, nothing useful can be inferred from it. It is not in fact a statement about value at all; it is a statement about language and how it is used in a particular society. Nevertheless, up this deeply-rutted garden path, Professor McFee leads us, pointing out items of interest along the way . . . the tribe which kills its sickly infants, the tribe which eats its aged parents; and so on, without pausing to wonder whether the conditions of group survival or the notion of filial homage might be one thing among the nomads of the Atlas Mountains or in a Brazilian rain forest, and quite another in the Home Counties. Certainly a tribe which believes it confers honour on its elders by eating them is going to be viewed askance by another which prefers to buy them a little bungalow somewhere, and Professor McFee should not be surprised that the notion of honour should manifest itself so differently in peoples so far removed in clime and in culture. What is surely more surprising is that notions such as honour should manifest themselves at all. For what *is* honour? What are pride, shame, fellow-feeling, generosity and love? If they are instincts, what are instincts? The prevailing temper of modern philosophy is to treat the instinct as a sort of terminus for any train of thought that seeks to trace our impulses to their origins. But what can be said to be the impulse of a genuinely altruistic act? Hobbes might have answered self-esteem, but what is the attraction or the point in thinking better of oneself? What is *better*? A savage who elects to honour his father by eating him as opposed to disposing of the body in some – to him – ignominious way, for example by burying it in a teak box, is making an ethical choice in that he believes himself to be acting as a good savage ought to act. Whence comes this sense of some actions being better than others? – not more useful, or more convenient, or more popular, but simply pointlessly *better*? What, in short, is so good about *good*? Professor McFee succeeds only in showing us that in different situations different actions will be deemed, rightly or wrongly, to be conducive to that good which is independent of time and place and which is knowable but not nameable. It is not nameable because it is not another way of referring to this or that quality which we have decided is virtuous. It is not courage, and it is not honesty or loyalty or kindness. The irreducible fact of goodness is not implicit in one kind of action any more than in its opposite, but in the existence of a relationship between the two. It is the sense of comparisons being in order. (*Pause.*) Full stop.

(*Music! Lights! Dorothy Moore – in person!*

. . . In fact, a track from Dotty's record, playing in the bedroom, and DOTTY *singing and miming to it, as* BONES *leaves the bedroom, the opening of the door triggering off the scene.* GEORGE *also goes into the hall, where he meets* BONES. *We can't hear what they say because the music is loud.*

GEORGE *takes* BONES *downstage to the kitchen exit, and goes off with him.* DOTTY *continues to sway and mime: the song is* 'Sentimental Journey'.

The dead JUMPER *is where he fell.*

The front door opens and ARCHIE *enters, and stops just inside the door, almost closing it behind him. He stands listening – an impressive figure, exquisitely dressed: orchid in buttonhole, cigarette in long black holder, and everything which those details suggest. He carefully opens the door of the study. The* SECRETARY *looks up. She nods at him, but it is impossible to draw any conclusions from that.*

ARCHIE *withdraws, closing the door. He comes downstage and looks along the corridor into the kitchen wing. He returns to the front door and opens it wide.*

SEVEN JUMPERS *in yellow tracksuits enter smoothly.* SIX *enter the bedroom,* ARCHIE *opening the door for them.*

ONE JUMPER *goes downstage to watch the kitchen exit.*

In the bedroom, DOTTY *is surprised but pleased by the entry of* ARCHIE *and the* JUMPERS. *They have come to remove the body.*

The song dominates the whole scene. Nothing else can be heard, and its beat infects the business of removing the body, for DOTTY *continues to sway and snap her fingers as she moves about welcoming the troops, and the* JUMPERS *lightly respond, so that the effect is a little simple improvised choreography between the* JUMPERS *and* DOTTY.

ARCHIE *moves downstage, facing front, and like a magician about to demonstrate a trick, takes from his pocket a small square of material like a handkerchief, which he unfolds and unfolds and unfolds until it is a large plastic bag, six feet tall, which he gives to* TWO JUMPERS. *These* TWO *hold the mouth of the bag open at the door; as the climax of the 'dance' the* FOUR JUMPERS *throw the body into the bag: bag closes, bedroom door closes,* JUMPERS *moving smoothly, front door closes, and on the last beat of the song, only* ARCHIE *and* DOTTY *are left on stage.*)

Blackout.

End of Act One

ACT TWO

The bedroom is blacked out, but music still comes from it –
presumably the next track on the album. Only a minute or two have
passed.

    BONES *appears from the kitchen entrance. He is pushing a*
well-laden dinner-trolley in front of him. It has on it a covered
casserole dish, a bottle of wine in an ice bucket, two glasses, two
plates, two of everything . . . dinner for two, in fact, and very
elegant.

    He is followed by GEORGE *holding a couple of lettuce leaves and*
a carrot, which he nibbles absently.

GEORGE: What do you mean, 'What does he look like?' He
    looks like a rabbit with long legs.
    (*But* BONES *has stopped, listening to Dotty's voice, rather as a*
    man might pause in St Peter's on hearing choristers . . .)
BONES: That was it. . . . That was the one she was singing . . .
    I remember how her voice faltered, I saw the tears spring
    into her eyes, the sobs shaking her breast . . . and that
    awful laughing scream as they brought the curtain down on
    the first lady of the musical stage – never to rise again! Oh
    yes, there are many stars in the West End night, but there's
    only ever been one Dorothy Moore . . .
GEORGE: Yes, I must say I envy her that. There have not
    been so many philosophers, but *two* of them have been
    George Moore, and it tends to dissipate the impact of
    one's name. But for that, I think my book *Conceptual*
    Problems of Knowledge and Mind would have caused quite
    a stir.
BONES: Any chance of a come-back, sir?
GEORGE: Well, I'm still hoping to find a publisher for it. I have
    also made a collection of my essays under the title,
    Language, Truth and God. An American publisher has
    expressed an interest but he wants to edit it himself and
    change the title to *You Better Believe It* . . . I suppose it

would be no worse than benefiting from my wife's gramophone records.

BONES: A consummate artist, sir. I felt it deeply when she retired.

GEORGE: Unfortunately she retired from consummation about the same time as she retired from artistry.

BONES: It was a personal loss, really.

GEORGE: Quite. She just went off it. I don't know why.

BONES: (*Coming round to him at last*) You don't have to explain to me, sir. You can't keep much from her die-hard fans. Actually, I had a brother who had a nervous breakdown. It's a terrible thing. It's the pressure, you know. The appalling pressure of being a star.

GEORGE: Was your brother a star?

BONES: No, he was an osteopath. Bones the Bones, they called him. Every patient had to make a little joke. It drove him mad, finally.

(*They have been approaching the bedroom door, but* BONES *suddenly abandons the trolley and takes* GEORGE *downstage. Earnestly.*) You see, Dorothy is a delicate creature, like a lustrous-eyed little bird you could hold in your hand, feeling its little brittle bones through its velvety skin – vulnerable, you understand; highly strung. No wonder she broke under the strain. And you don't get over it, just like that. It can go on for years, the effect, afterwards – building up again, underneath, until, one day – *Snap!* – do something violent perhaps, quite out of character, you know what I mean? It would be like a blackout. She wouldn't know what she was doing. (*He grips* GEORGE's *elbow.*) And I should think that any competent or, better still, eminent psychiatric expert witness would be prepared to say so. Of course, he wouldn't be cheap, but it can be done, do you follow me?

GEORGE: (*Puzzled*) I'm not sure that I do.

BONES: Well, your wife says you can explain everything, and you say you are wholly responsible, but –

GEORGE: Are you still going on about that? – for goodness sake,

I just lost my temper for a moment, that's all, and took matters into my own hands.

BONES: Because of the noise?

GEORGE: Exactly.

BONES: Don't you think it was a bit extreme?

GEORGE: Yes, yes, I suppose it was a bit.

BONES: Won't wash, Wilfred. I believe you are trying to shield her.

GEORGE: Shield who?

BONES: It's quite understandable. Is there a man who could stand aside when this fair creature is in trouble –

GEORGE: Aren't you getting a little carried away? The point is, surely, that I'm the householder and I must be held responsible for what happens in my house.

BONES: I don't think the burden of being a householder extends to responsibility for any crime committed on the premises.

GEORGE: Crime? You call that a crime?

BONES: (*With more heat*) Well, what would you call it?

GEORGE: It was just a bit of *fun*! Where's your sense of humour, man?

BONES: (*Staggered*) I don't know, you bloody philosophers are all the same, aren't you? A man is dead and you're as cool as you like. Your wife begged me with tears in her eyes to go easy on you, and I don't mind admitting I was deeply moved –

GEORGE: Excuse me –

BONES: (*Angrily*) But you're wasted on her, mate. What on earth made *her* marry *you*, I'll never know, when there are so many better men – decent, strong, protective, understanding, sensitive –

GEORGE: Did you say somebody was dead?

BONES: Stone dead, in the bedroom.

GEORGE: Don't be ridiculous.

BONES: The body is lying on the floor!

GEORGE: (*Going to door*) You have obviously taken leave of your senses.

BONES: Don't touch it! – it will have to be examined for fingerprints.

GEORGE: If there is a body on the floor, it will have my *footprints* on it.

(*He opens the bedroom door. In the bedroom, no one is in view. The drapes – or screens – are round the bed. An ambiguous machine – the dermatograph – is set up so that it peers with its lens through the drapes. Some camera-lights are in position round the bed, shining down over the drapes into the bed. The TV set is connected by a lead to the dermatograph.*

GEORGE *pauses in the doorway.*)

ARCHIE: (*Within*) . . . There . . .

DOTTY: (*Within*) . . . Yes . . .

ARCHIE: There . . . there . . .

DOTTY: Yes . . .

ARCHIE: . . . and there . . .

DOTTY: Yes . . . yes.

(*These sounds are consistent with a proper doctor–patient relationship. If* DOTTY *has a tendency to gasp slightly it is probably because the stethoscope is cold.* ARCHIE *on the other hand, might be getting rather overheated under the blaze of the dermatograph lights.*)

ARCHIE: (*Within*) Excuse me . . .

(*Archie's coat comes sailing over the drapes.* GEORGE *retreats, closing the door.*)

GEORGE: Well, he's very much alive now.

(*On this bitter note,* GEORGE *goes into the study.* BONES, *with the trolley, cautiously enters the bedroom. No one is in view.* BONES *pauses. One of Archie's shoes comes over the drapes and falls on the floor. Another pause. The second shoe comes over, falling into* BONES's *hands. The absence of a thump brings* ARCHIE's *head into view, popping up over the drapes.*)

ARCHIE: Ah! Good morning!

(ARCHIE *moves to come out from the bed. Meanwhile* DOTTY *looks over the top.*)

DOTTY: Lunch! And Bonesy!

(ARCHIE *picks his coat up and hands it to* BONES, *and then readies himself to put his arms in the sleeves, as though* BONES *were a manservant.*)

ARCHIE: (*Slipping on his coat*) Thank you so much. Rather warm in there. The lights, you know.

DOTTY: Isn't he sweet?

ARCHIE: Charming. What happened to Mrs Whatsername?

DOTTY: No, no, it's Bonesy!

BONES: Inspector Bones, CID.

DOTTY: (*Disappearing*) Excuse me!

ARCHIE: Bones. . . ? I had a patient named Bones. I wonder if he was any relation? – an osteopath.

BONES: My brother!

ARCHIE: Remember the case well. Cognomen Syndrome. My advice to him was to take his wife's maiden name of Foot and carry on from there.

BONES: He took your advice but unfortunately he got interested in chiropody. He is now in an asylum near Uxbridge.

ARCHIE: Isn't that interesting? I must write him up. The Cognomen Syndrome is my baby, you know.

BONES: You discovered it?

ARCHIE: I've got it. Jumper's the name – my card.

BONES: (*Reading off card*) 'Sir Archibald Jumper, MD, DPhil, DLitt, LD, DPM, DPT (*Gym*)'. . . . What's all that?

ARCHIE: I'm a doctor of medicine, philosophy, literature and law, with diplomas in psychological medicine and PT including gym.

BONES: (*Handing back the card*) I see that you are the Vice-Chancellor of Professor Moore's university.

ARCHIE: Not a bad record, is it? And I can still jump over seven feet.

BONES: High jump?

ARCHIE: Long jump. My main interest, however, is the trampoline.

BONES: Mine is show business generally.

ARCHIE: Really? Well, nowadays, of course, I do more theory than practice, but if trampoline acts appeal to you at all, a vacancy has lately occurred in a little team I run, mainly for our own amusement with a few social engagements thrown in –

BONES: Just a minute, just a minute! – What happened to Professor McFee?

ARCHIE: Exactly. I regret to tell you he is dead.

BONES: I realize he is *dead* –

ARCHIE: Shocking tragedy. I am entirely to blame.

BONES: You, too, sir?

ARCHIE: Yes, Inspector.

BONES: Very chivalrous, sir, but I'm afraid it won't wash. (*He addresses the drapes, loudly.*) Miss Moore, is there anything you wish to say at this stage?

DOTTY: (*Her head appearing*) Sorry?

BONES: My dear – we are all *sorry* –
(DOTTY *disappears.*)

ARCHIE: Just a moment! I will not have a patient of mine brow-beaten by the police.

BONES: (*Thoughtfully*) Patient . . .

ARCHIE: Yes. As you can see I have been taking a dermatographical reading.

BONES: (*Indicating the dermatograph*) This? What does it do?

ARCHIE: It reads the skin, electronically; hence dermatograph. All kinds of disturbances under the skin show up on the surface, if we can learn to read it, and we are learning.

BONES: Disturbances? Mental disturbances?

ARCHIE: Among other things.

BONES: (*A new intimacy*) Sir Jim –

ARCHIE: Archie –

BONES: Sir Archie, might I have a word with you, in private?

ARCHIE: Just what I was about to suggest. (*He opens the bedroom door.*) Shall we step outside. . . ?
(BONES *steps into the hall.*)

DOTTY: . . . Things don't seem so bad after all. So to speak.
(ARCHIE *follows* BONES *into the hall. Fade out on bedroom.* ARCHIE *and* BONES *move towards kitchen exit.*)

BONES: This is just between you and me, Sigmund. I understand your feelings only too well. What decent man could stand aside while that beautiful, frail creature –

ARCHIE: Let's come to the point, Inspector. The plain facts are that while performing some modest acrobatics for the entertainment of Miss Moore's party-guests, Professor McFee was killed by a bullet fired from the outer darkness.

We all saw him shot, but none of us saw who shot him. With the possible exception of McFee's fellow gymnasts, anybody could have fired the shot, and anybody could have had a reason for doing so, including, incidentally, myself.

BONES: And what might *your* motive be, sir?

ARCHIE: Who knows? Perhaps McFee, my faithful protégé, had secretly turned against me, gone off the rails and decided that he was St Paul to Moore's Messiah.

BONES: Doesn't seem much of a reason.

ARCHIE: It depends. Moore himself is not important – he is our tame believer, pointed out to visitors in much the same spirit as we point out the magnificent stained glass in what is now the gymnasium. But McFee was the guardian and figurehead of philosophical orthodoxy, and if he threatened to start calling on his masters to return to the true path, then I'm afraid it would certainly have been an ice-pick in the back of the skull.

DOTTY: (*Off*) Darling!

ARCHIE: And then again, perhaps it was Dorothy. Or someone. (*Smiles.*)

DOTTY: (*Off*) Darling!

BONES: My advice to you is, number one, get her lawyer over here –

ARCHIE: That will not be necessary. I am Miss Moore's legal adviser.

BONES: Number two, completely off the record, get her off on expert evidence – nervous strain, appalling pressure, and one day – snap! – blackout, can't remember a thing. Put her in the box and you're half-way there. The other half is, get something on Mad Jock McFee, and if you don't get a Scottish judge it'll be three years' probation and the sympathy of the court.

ARCHIE: This is most civil of you, Inspector, but a court appearance would be most embarrassing to my client and patient; and three years' probation is not an insignificant curtailment of a person's liberty.

BONES: For God's sake, man, we're talking about a murder charge.

54

ARCHIE: You are. What I had in mind is that McFee, suffering from nervous strain brought on by the appalling pressure of overwork – for which I blame myself entirely – left here last night in a mood of deep depression, and wandered into the park, where he crawled into a large plastic bag and shot himself . . .

(*Pause.* BONES *opens his mouth to speak.*)

. . . leaving this note . . . (ARCHIE *produces it from his pocket.*) . . . which was found in the bag together with his body by some gymnasts on an early morning keep-fit run.

(*Pause.* BONES *opens his mouth to speak.*)

Here is the coroner's certificate.

(ARCHIE *produces another note, which* BONES *takes from him.* BONES *reads it.*)

BONES: Is this genuine?

ARCHIE: (*Testily*) Of course it's genuine. I'm a coroner, not a forger.

(BONES *hands the certificate back, and almost comes to attention.*)

BONES: Sir Archibald Bouncer –

ARCHIE: Jumper.

BONES: Sir Archibald Jumper, I must –

ARCHIE: Now, I judge from your curiously formal and somewhat dated attitude, that you are deaf to offers of large sums of money.

BONES: I didn't hear that.

ARCHIE: Exactly. On the other hand, I think you are a man who feels that his worth has not been recognized. Other men have got on – younger men, flashier men . . . Superintendents . . . Commissioners . . .

BONES: There may be something in that.

ARCHIE: I dare say your ambitions do not stop with the Police Force, even.

BONES: Oh?

ARCHIE: Inspector, my patronage is not extensive, but it is select. I can offer prestige, the respect of your peers and almost unlimited credit among the local shopkeepers – in short, the Chair of Divinity is yours for the asking.

BONES: The Chair of Divinity?

ARCHIE: Not perhaps, the Chair which is in the eye of the hurricane nowadays, but a professorship will still be regarded as a distinction come the day – early next week, in all probability – when the Police Force will be thinned out to a ceremonial front for the peace-keeping activities of the Army.

BONES: I see. Well, until that happens, I should still like to know – if McFee shot himself inside a plastic bag, where is the gun?

ARCHIE: (*Awed*) Very good thinking indeed! On consideration I can give you the Chair of Logic, but that is my last offer.

BONES: This is a British murder inquiry and some degree of justice must be seen to be more or less done.

ARCHIE: I must say I find your attitude lacking in flexibility. What makes you so sure that it *was* Miss Moore who shot McFee?

BONES: I have a nose for these things.

ARCHIE: With the best will in the world I can't give the Chair of Logic to a man who relies on nasal intuition.

DOTTY: (*Off*) Help!

(BONES *reacts*. ARCHIE *restrains him*.)

ARCHIE: It's all right – just exhibitionism: what we psychiatrists call 'a cry for help'.

BONES: But it *was* a cry for help.

ARCHIE: Perhaps I'm not making myself clear. *All* exhibitionism is a cry for help, but a cry for help *as such* is only exhibitionism.

DOTTY: (*Off*) MURDER!

(BONES *rushes to the bedroom, which remains dark*. ARCHIE *looks at his watch and leaves towards the kitchen. In the study,* GEORGE *resumes*.)

GEORGE: The study of moral philosophy is an attempt to determine what we mean when we say that something is good and that something else is bad. Not all value judgements, however, are the proper study of the moral philosopher. Language is a finite instrument crudely applied to an infinity of ideas, and one consequence of the failure to take account of this is that modern philosophy has made itself ridiculous by analysing such statements as, 'This is a good bacon sandwich,' or, 'Bedser had a good wicket.' (*The* SECRETARY *raises her head at 'Bedser'.*) Bedser! – Good God. B-E-D-S-E-R.

Likewise, to say that this is a good bacon sandwich is only to say that by the criteria applied by like-minded lovers of bacon sandwiches, this one is worthy of approbation. The word good is reducible to other properties such as crisp, lean and unadulterated by tomato sauce. You will have seen at once that to a man who likes his bacon sandwiches underdone, fatty and smothered in ketchup, this would be a rather *poor* bacon sandwich. By subjecting any given example to similar analysis, the modern school, in which this university has played so lamentable a part, has satisfied itself that all statements implying goodness or badness, whether in conduct or in bacon sandwiches, are not statements of *fact* but merely expressions of feeling, taste or vested interest.

But when we say that the Good Samaritan acted well, we are surely expressing more than a circular prejudice about behaviour. We mean he acted kindly – selflessly – *well*. And what is our approval of kindness based on if not on the intuition that kindness is simply good in itself and cruelty is not. A man who sees that he is about to put his foot down on a beetle in his path, decides to step on it or not to. Why? What process is at work? And what is that quick blind mindless connection suddenly made and lost by the man who didn't see the beetle but only heard the crunch? (*Towards the end of this speech,* ARCHIE *re-enters and quietly lets himself into the study.*)

It is ironic that the school which denies the claims of the intuition to know good when it sees it, is itself the product of the pioneer work set out in his *Principia Ethica* by the late G. E. Moore, an intuitionist philosopher whom I respected from afar but who, whether or not from intuition, was never in when I called. Moore did not believe in God, but I do not hold that against him – for of all forms of wishful thinking, humanism demands the greatest sympathy – and at least by insisting that goodness was a fact, and on his right to recognize it when he saw it, Moore avoided the moral limbo devised by his successors, who are in the unhappy position of having to admit that one man's idea of good is no more meaningful than another man's whether he be St Francis or – Vice-Chancellor!

(*For he has noticed* ARCHIE. ARCHIE *comes forward.*)

ARCHIE: An inept comparison, if I may say so. I too am very fond of animals. (*He picks up* PAT.) What do you call it?

GEORGE: Pat.

ARCHIE: Pat! . . . what a lovely name.

GEORGE: It's a good name for a tortoise, being sexually ambiguous. I also have a hare called Thumper, somewhere. . . . By the way, I wasn't really comparing St Francis with you.

ARCHIE: Quite understand. You were going to say Hitler or Stalin or Nero . . . the argument always gets back to some lunatic tyrant, the *reductio ad absurdum* of the new ethics, and the dog-eared trump card of the intuitionists.

GEORGE: (*Rising to that*) Well, why not? When I push *my* convictions to absurdity, *I* arrive at God – which is at least as embarrassing nowadays. (*Pause.*) All I know is that I think that I know that I know that nothing can be created out of nothing, that my moral conscience is different from the rules of my tribe, and that there is more in me than meets the microscope – and because of *that* I'm saddled with this incredible, indescribable and definitely shifty *God*, the trump card of atheism.

ARCHIE: It's always been a mystery to me why religious faith and atheism should be thought of as opposing attitudes.

GEORGE: Always?

ARCHIE: It just occurred to me.

GEORGE: It occurred to you that belief in God and the conviction that God doesn't exist amount to much the same thing?

ARCHIE: It gains from careful phrasing. Religious faith and atheism differ mainly about God; about Man they are in accord: Man is the highest form of life, he has duties he has rights, etcetera, and it is usually better to be kind than cruel. Even if there is some inscrutable divinity behind it all, our condition for good or ill is apparently determined by our choice of actions, and choosing seems to be a genuine human possibility. Indeed, it is surely religious zeal rather than atheism which is historically notorious in the fortunes of mankind.

GEORGE: I'm not at all sure that the God of religious observance is the object of my faith. Do you suppose it would be presumptuous to coin a deity?

ARCHIE: I don't see the point. If he caught on, you'd kill for him, too. (*Suddenly remembering.*) Ah! – I knew there was something! – McFee's dead.

GEORGE: What?!!

ARCHIE: Shot himself this morning, in the park, in a plastic bag.

GEORGE: My God! Why?

ARCHIE: It's hard to say. He was always tidy.

GEORGE: But to shoot himself . . .

ARCHIE: Oh, he could be very violent, you know . . . In fact we had a furious row last night – perhaps the Inspector had asked you about that. . . ?

GEORGE: No . . .

ARCHIE: It was a purely trivial matter. He took offence at my description of Edinburgh as the Reykjavik of the South. (GEORGE *is not listening.*)

GEORGE: . . . Where did he find the despair. . . ? I thought the whole *point* of denying the Absolute was to reduce the scale, instantly, to the inconsequential behaviour of inconsequential animals; that nothing could ever be that important . . .

ARCHIE: Including, I suppose, death . . . It's an interesting view of atheism, as a sort of *crutch* for those who can't bear the reality of God . . .

GEORGE: (*Still away*) I wonder if McFee was afraid of death? And if he was, what was it that he would have been afraid of: surely not the chemical change in the material that was his body. I suppose he would have said, as so many do, that it is only the dying he feared, yes, the physical process of giving out. But it's not the dying with me – one knows about pain. It's *death* that I'm afraid of.

(*Pause.*)

ARCHIE: Incidentally, since his paper has of course been circulated to everyone, it must remain the basis of the symposium.

GEORGE: Yes, indeed, I have spent weeks preparing my commentary on it.

ARCHIE: We shall begin with a two-minute silence. That will give me a chance to prepare mine.

GEORGE: You will be replying, Vice-Chancellor?

ARCHIE: At such short notice I don't see who else could stand in. I'll relinquish the chair, of course, and we'll get a caretaker to take my place, someone of good standing; he won't have to know much philosophy. Just enough for a tribute to Duncan.

GEORGE: Poor McFee . . . I like to think he'll be there in spirit.

ARCHIE: If only to make sure the materialistic argument is properly represented.

DOTTY: (*Off*) Darling!

(*Both men respond automatically, and both halt and look at each other.*)

GEORGE &
ARCHIE: } How is she?

GEORGE: How do I know? You're the doctor.

ARCHIE: That's true.

(ARCHIE *moves out of the study,* GEORGE *with him; into the hall.*)

I naturally try to get her to open up, but one can't assume she tells me everything, or even that it's the truth.

GEORGE: Well, I don't know what's the matter with her. She's like a cat on hot bricks, and doesn't emerge from her room. All she says is, she's all right in bed.

ARCHIE: Yes, well there's something in that.

GEORGE: (*Restraining his going; edgily*) What exactly do you do in there?

60

ARCHIE: Therapy takes many forms.

GEORGE: I had no idea you were still practising.

ARCHIE: Oh yes . . . a bit of law, a bit of philosophy, a bit of medicine, a bit of gym . . . A bit of one and then a bit of the other.

GEORGE: You examine her?

ARCHIE: Oh yes, I like to keep my hand in. You must understand, my dear Moore, that when I'm examining Dorothy I'm not a lawyer or a philosopher. Or a gymnast, of course. Oh, I know, my dear fellow – you think that when I'm examining Dorothy I see her eyes as cornflowers, her lips as rubies, her skin as soft and warm as velvet – you think that when I run my hands over her back I am carried away by the delicate contours that flow like a sea-shore from shoulder to heel – oh yes, you think my mind turns to ripe pears as soon as I press –

GEORGE: (*Viciously*) No, I don't!

ARCHIE: But to us medical men, the human body is just an imperfect machine. As it is to most of us philosophers. And to us gymnasts, of course.

DOTTY: (*Off*) Ready . . .

(ARCHIE *smiles at* GEORGE, *and quickly lets himself into the bedroom, closing the door behind him.*
The bedroom lights up. The dermatograph and the lights have been put away. The bed is revealed as before. BONES *is wearing a frock, a headdress, and black-face. He is using a wastebin as a bongo drum.*)

Black Beauty?

BONES: No, it's a film.

(BONES *does an African war-cry.*)

DOTTY: Zulu's back in town!?

BONES: No, no. (*He minces about.*)

DOTTY: The African Queen!

BONES: That's the one!

(DOTTY *squeals with delight.* ARCHIE *has entered the bedroom and is standing behind* BONES.)

ARCHIE: Tush . . . tush, Inspector. I am shocked . . . deeply shocked.

BONES: No – no – no – I was just . . .

ARCHIE: What will they say back at the station?

BONES: No – no – we were just . . .

ARCHIE: What a tragic end to an incorruptible career.

BONES: No – please!

ARCHIE: Do not despair. I'm sure we can come to some arrangement.

(*Lights cross-fade to the study.*)

GEORGE: How the hell does one know what to believe?

(*The* SECRETARY *has taken down the last sentence.*)

No, no – (*Changes mind.*) Well, all right. (*Dictating*) How does one know what it is one believes when it's so difficult to know what it is one knows. I don't claim to *know* that God exists, I only claim that he does without my knowing it, and while I claim as much I do not claim to know as much; indeed I cannot know and God knows I cannot. (*Pause.*) And yet I tell you that, now and again, not necessarily in the contemplation of rainbows or newborn babes, nor in extremities of pain or joy, but more probably ambushed by some quite trivial moment – say the exchange of signals between two long-distance lorry-drivers in the black sleet of a god-awful night on the old A1 – then, in that dip-flash, dip-flash of headlights in the rain that seems to affirm some common ground that is not animal and not long-distance lorry-driving – then I tell you I *know* – I sound like a joke vicar, new paragraph.

There is in mathematics a concept known as a limiting curve, that is the curve defined as the limit of a polygon with an infinite number of sides. For example, if I had never seen a circle and didn't know how to draw one, I could nevertheless postulate the existence of circles by thinking of them as regular polygons with numberless edges, so that an old threepenny-bit would be a bumpy imperfect circle which would approach perfection if I kept doubling the number of its sides: at infinity the result would be the circle which I have never seen and do not know how to draw, and which is logically implied by the existence of polygons. And now and again, not necessarily in the contemplation of polygons or newborn babes, nor in extremities of pain or joy, but more probably in some quite trivial moment, it seems to me that life itself is the mundane figure which argues perfection at its limiting curve. And if I doubt it, the ability to doubt, to question, to *think*, seems to be the curve itself. *Cogito ergo deus est.* (*Pause.*) The fact that I cut a ludicrous figure in the academic world is largely due to my aptitude for reducing a complex and logical thesis to a mysticism of staggering banality. McFee never made that mistake, never put himself at risk by finding mystery in the clockwork, never looked for trouble or over his shoulder, and I'm sorry he's gone but what can be his complaint? McFee jumped, and left nothing behind but a vacancy. (*Pause.*) A vacancy . . . (*There is a delicious laugh from* DOTTY *in the dark.* GEORGE *strides out of the study; then the bedroom is lit.* ARCHIE *and* DOTTY *are sitting at the trolley eating a very civilized lunch.* BONES *has gone.*)

DOTTY: I must say, I do find mashed potatoes and gravy very consoling.

(GEORGE *enters without knocking.*)

GEORGE: I'm sorry to interrupt your inquiries –

(*He looks round for the Inspector.*

ARCHIE *smoothly takes a silver-backed notebook from his pocket, and a silver pencil from another.*)

ARCHIE: When did you first become aware of these feelings?

DOTTY: (*Gaily*) I don't know – I've *always* found mashed potatoes and gravy very consoling.

GEORGE: Where's the Inspector?

ARCHIE: The inquiries have been completed. Did you want him?

GEORGE: Well no . . . As a matter of fact, I came to ask you . . . Vice-Chancellor, about the Chair of Logic.

(GEORGE *is unsettled by the lunch-party atmosphere. Nothing about* ARCHIE *or* DOTTY *suggests that there is anything unusual about it. They continue to eat and drink.*)

ARCHIE: Yes?

GEORGE: You probably have had very little time to think about McFee's successor . . .

ARCHIE: The appointment to the Chair of Logic is of course a matter for the gravest consideration. We've always been a happy team and I shall be looking for someone who will fit in, someone with a bit of bounce.

GEORGE: Yes. Well, it just seemed to me that as the senior professor –

ARCHIE: The oldest –

GEORGE: The longest-serving professor –

ARCHIE: Oh yes.

GEORGE: Well, Logic has traditionally been considered the senior Chair . . .

ARCHIE: (*Pause*) Yes, well, there you are; you have made your request. But I'm not too happy about your Ethics.

GEORGE: I'm not seeking any favours –

ARCHIE: No, no, I mean Ethics. Ethics has always been your department – what will happen to Ethics?

GEORGE: There's no conflict there. My work on moral philosophy has always been based on logical principles, and it would do no harm at all if the Chair of Logic applied itself occasionally to the activities of the human race.

ARCHIE: Yes . . . yes . . . But you see, the Chair of Logic is considered the leading edge of philosophical inquiry here, and *your* strong point is, how shall I put it, well, many of the students are under the impression that you are the author of *Principia Ethica*.

GEORGE: But he's been dead for years.

ARCHIE: That is why I take a serious view of the mistake.

GEORGE: (*Pause*) I see. (*Moves towards door.*) Incidentally, what do you psychiatrists call *this* form of therapy?

ARCHIE: Lunch. I don't wish to make a habit of denying you chairs, but you will appreciate that I can't ask you to sit down – a psychiatrist is akin to a priest taking confession.

DOTTY: Well, it wasn't *me*.

ARCHIE: Absolute privacy, absolute trust.

DOTTY: *I* didn't do it. I thought *you* did it.

GEORGE: What is she talking about? Where's the Inspector?

DOTTY: He's gone. I never saw a man so changed, for a plainclothes detective.

GEORGE: Without taking his record?

DOTTY: Oh yes, we must send it on.

(GEORGE *can't put his finger on it, but something is bothering him. He starts to wander towards the bathroom.*)

GEORGE: I'm surprised he just . . . went . . . like that.

(GEORGE *enters the bathroom.*)

(*Off; horrified*) My *God!*

(GEORGE *enters from the bathroom, white, shaking with rage.*)

You murderous *bitch!* . . . You might have put some water in the bath!

(*He is holding a dead goldfish.*)

DOTTY: Oh dear . . . I am sorry. I forgot about it.

GEORGE: Poor little Archie – (*Catches himself.*)

(ARCHIE *raises his head a fraction.*)

Murdered for a charade!

DOTTY: (*Angrily*) Murdered? Don't you dare splash *me* with your sentimental rhetoric! It's a bloody goldfish! Do you think every *sole meunière* comes to you untouched by suffering?

GEORGE: The monk who won't walk in the garden for fear of treading on an ant does not have to be a vegetarian . . . There is an irrational difference which has a rational value.

DOTTY: Brilliant! You must publish your findings in some suitable place like the *Good Food Guide.* You bloody humbug! – the last of the metaphysical egocentrics! You're probably still shaking from the four-hundred-year-old news that the sun doesn't go round *you!*

GEORGE: We are *all* still shaking. Copernicus cracked our confidence, and Einstein smashed it: for if one can no longer believe that a twelve-inch ruler is always a foot long, how can one be sure of relatively less certain propositions, such as that God made the Heaven and the Earth . . .

DOTTY: (*Dry, drained*) Well, it's all over now. Not only are we no longer the still centre of God's universe, we're not even uniquely graced by his footprint in man's image . . . Man is on the Moon, his feet on solid ground, and he has seen us whole, all in one go, *little – local* . . . and all our absolutes, the thou-shalts and the thou-shalt-nots that seemed to be the very condition of our existence, how did *they* look to two moonmen with a single neck to save between them? Like the local customs of another place. When that thought drips through to the bottom, people won't just carry on. There is going to be such . . . breakage, such gnashing of unclean meats, such coveting of neighbours' oxen and knowing of neighbours' wives, such dishonourings of mothers and fathers, and bowings and scrapings to images graven and incarnate, such killing of goldfish and maybe more – (*Looks up, tear-stained.*) Because the truths that have been taken on trust, they've never had edges before, there was no vantage point to stand on and see where they stopped. (*And weeps.*)

ARCHIE: (*Pause*) When did you first become aware of these feelings?

DOTTY: Georgie . . .

  (*But* GEORGE *won't or can't . . .*)

GEORGE: (*Facing away, out front, emotionless*) Meeting a friend in a corridor, Wittgenstein said: 'Tell me, why do people always say it was *natural* for men to assume that the sun went round the earth rather than that the earth was rotating?' His friend said, 'Well, obviously, because it just *looks* as if the sun is going round the earth.' To which the philosopher replied, 'Well, what would it have looked like if it had looked as if the earth was rotating?'

ARCHIE: I really can't conduct a consultation under these conditions! You might as well join us.

GEORGE: (*Moving*) No, thank you.

ARCHIE: Do . . . This, whatever it is, makes a very good casserole.

DOTTY: (*Dry-eyed revenge*) It's not casseroled. It's jugged.
  (GEORGE *freezes. Pause.*
  Doorbell.)

GEORGE: Dorothy . . .

DOTTY: Somebody at the door.
  (*It's* CROUCH, *who rings the bell out of formality and lets himself in with his master key, pausing in the door so as not to intrude on anything, announcing himself:* 'Crouch!')

GEORGE: Dorothy . . . You *didn't*. . . ?

CROUCH: Hello!

(*He closes the front door behind him.*

GEORGE *turns abruptly and walks swiftly out, to his study. In the hall he passes by* CROUCH.)

Excuse me, sir. . . .

GEORGE: (*Shouts viciously*) You seem to be taking out the rubbish at any time that suits you!!

(CROUCH *is dumbfounded.*

GEORGE *walks into the study, leaving the door open, and slumps into his chair.*

The SECRETARY *is patient and discreet.*

CROUCH *timidly enters the study.*)

CROUCH: I haven't come for the rubbish, sir.

GEORGE: I'm sorry, Mr Crouch . . . I'm very sorry. I was upset. It's just been the most awful day.

(*He comforts himself with the tortoise.*)

CROUCH: I quite understand, sir. I'm upset myself. I just came up to see if there was anything I could do, I knew you'd be upset. . . .

(GEORGE *looks at him.*)

I got to know him quite well, you know . . . made quite a friend of him.

GEORGE: You knew about it?

CROUCH: I was there, sir. Doing the drinks. It shocked me, I can tell you.

GEORGE: Who killed him?

CROUCH: Well, I wouldn't like to say for certain . . . I mean, I heard a bang, and when I looked, there he was crawling on the ground . . .

(GEORGE *winces.*)

. . . and there was Miss Moore . . . well –

GEORGE: Do you realize she's in there now, *eating* him?

CROUCH: (*Pause*) You mean – *raw*?

GEORGE: (*Crossly*) No, of course not! – *cooked* – with gravy and mashed potatoes.

CROUCH: (*Pause*) I thought she was on the mend, sir.

GEORGE: Do you think I'm being too sentimental about the whole thing?

CROUCH: (*Firmly*) I do not, sir. I think it's a police matter.

GEORGE: Yes! No – They'd laugh at me . . . There *was* a policeman here, but he's gone.

CROUCH: Yes, sir, I saw him leave. I thought that would be him. You were wondering, sir, who brought them round.

GEORGE: No. I telephoned them myself.

CROUCH: You're an honest man, sir. In the circumstances I don't mind telling you I also phoned them myself, anonymous.

GEORGE: Did you? . . . Well, it's all right now, he's gone. Lot of fuss about nothing. I know things got a bit out of hand but . . . I'm surprised at your puritanism, Mr Crouch. . . . A little wine, women and song . . .

CROUCH: Yes, sir. Of course, it was the murder of Professor McFee that was the main thing.

(*Long pause.* GEORGE *sits perfectly still, and continues to do so, sightless, deaf, while* CROUCH *speaks.*)

By the way, sir. . . . (*Picking up the tortoise.*) I hope you don't mind my taking the opportunity, but as you know, no pets allowed in the flats – I don't mind turning a blind eye to this little fellow, but I've seen a rabbit around the place of a morning, and it's as much as my job's worth – I hope you don't mind, sir . . . (*Pause.*) Will Miss Moore be . . . leaving, sir?

GEORGE: (*Blinking awake*) She's in bed with the doctor.

(*Small pause. He jumps up and strides into the bedroom.* ARCHIE *and* DOTTY *are calmly watching the TV. The big screen shows us what they see – the read-back of Dotty's naked body.*)

Crouch says – (*He is momentarily taken aback by the fact that they are watching TV*) – Crouch says –

(ARCHIE *and* DOTTY *go 'Sssssh!' and continue to watch the screen.*)

(*Advancing*) Crouch says –

(*Then* GEORGE *sees the TV and the naked body on it. He pauses: the body is familiar to him, perhaps.*)

What's going on?

ARCHIE: The dermatograph, you know. All kinds of disturbances under the skin show up on the surface, if we can learn to read it, and we –

GEORGE: (*Abruptly turning off the set, so that the big screen goes blank*) You must think I'm a bloody fool!

ARCHIE: What do you mean?

GEORGE: Well, everything you do makes it *look* as if you're . . . (*Pause.*)

ARCHIE: Well, what would it have *looked* like if it had *looked* as if I were making a dermatographical examination?

DOTTY: What's the matter, Georgie?

GEORGE: Dotty . . .

DOTTY: Don't take any notice of Archie – him and his ripe pears!

GEORGE: Crouch says McFee was shot! – here – last night – He thinks Dorothy did it –

DOTTY: I thought Archie did it. *You* didn't do it, did you, Georgie? (*She pulls the sheet over her head.*)

GEORGE: Dorothy – don't hide – it's not a charade. Crouch says he *saw* – For God's sake – I don't know what to do –

ARCHIE: Crouch says he saw *what*, George?

GEORGE: Well, he didn't actually *see* . . .

ARCHIE: Quite. We just don't *know*.

GEORGE: There are many things I know which are not verifiable but nobody can tell me I don't know them, and I think that I know that something happened to poor Dotty and she somehow killed McFee, as sure as she killed my poor Thumper.

DOTTY: Georgie . . . it was only a joke.

(GEORGE *leaves the bedroom and* ARCHIE *follows him out. The bedroom blacks out. They both walk into the study where* CROUCH *is seated at George's desk, reading the typescript and chuckling.*)

CROUCH: Saint Sebastian died of fright! – very good! (*To* SECRETARY; *surprisingly.*) Of course, the flaw in the argument *is* that even if the first term of his infinitely regressing series is zero rather than infinitesimal, the original problem remains in identifying the *second* term of

the series, which however small must be *greater* than zero –
you take my point? I grant you he's answered Russell's first
point, I grant you that – the smallest proper fraction is zero
– *but* –
(GEORGE *snatches the paper from behind* CROUCH *and studies
it minutely, already talking.*)

GEORGE: Yes, but you entirely miss *my* point, which is that
having established that the first term – that is God –
corresponds to zero, there's no need to worry about the
second term – it is enough that it *is* the second – Surely you
can see that?

CROUCH: (*Humbly*) I expect you're right, sir. I mean, it's only a
hobby with me.

ARCHIE: (*Coming forard*) Mr Crouch!

CROUCH: Oh, good morning, Vice-Chancellor, sir . . .
(*The situation:* CROUCH *and* ARCHIE *conversing out of the
study into the hall.* GEORGE *worrying his script. The*
SECRETARY *still the observer with pencil and pad ready. Once
in the hall,* ARCHIE *shuts the study door.*)

ARCHIE: I see you're something of a philosopher, Mr Crouch.

CROUCH: Oh, I wouldn't call it that, sir – I just picked up a bit
. . . a bit of reading, a bit of chatting, you know.

ARCHIE: Isn't that the academic life? Whom would you describe
as your mentor?

CROUCH: It was the late Professor McFee.

ARCHIE: Really?

CROUCH: Yes, sir, it was a terrible thing, his death. Of course,
his whole life was going through a crisis, as he no doubt
told you.

ARCHIE: Yes. . . ?

CROUCH: It was the astronauts fighting on the Moon that finally
turned him, sir. Henry, he said to me, Henry, I am giving
philosophical respectability to a new pragmatism in public
life, of which there have been many disturbing examples
both here and on the Moon. Duncan, I said, Duncan, don't
let it get you down, have another can of beer. But he kept
harking back to the first Captain Oates, out there in the
Antarctic wastes, sacrificing his life to give his companions

70

a slim chance of survival . . . Henry, he said, what made him do it? – out of the tent and into the jaws of the blizzard. If altruism is a possibility, he said, my argument is up a gum-tree . . . Duncan, I said, Duncan, don't you worry your head about all that. That astronaut yobbo is good for twenty years hard. Yes, he said, yes *maybe*, but when he comes out, he's going to find he was only twenty years ahead of his time. I have seen the future, Henry, he said; and it's yellow.

ARCHIE: (*Pause*) You must have been a close friend of his. (*From now on, for the following speeches, the* SECRETARY *is the only person moving on stage. She gets up. She gets her coat out of the wardrobe. She is going to go for lunch. Perhaps a clock has struck.*)

CROUCH: Ah, well, he'd come by to pick up his girl.

ARCHIE: His girl?

CROUCH: And he was always a bit early and as often as not Professor Moore kept her working a bit late.

ARCHIE: Professor Moore?

CROUCH: So he'd pass the time with me . . . I shall miss our little talks. And of course it's tragic for her. I see she's carrying on, losing herself in her work; it's the only way . . . but after three years of secret betrothal, it takes a certain kind of girl.

ARCHIE: Yes. Why secret?

CROUCH: He made her keep it secret because of his wife.

ARCHIE: Ah. His wife didn't know, of course.

CROUCH: His wife knew about *her*, but *she* didn't know about his wife. He was *terrified* to tell her, poor Duncan. Well, he won't be coming round here any more. Not that he would have done anyway, of course.

ARCHIE: Why's that?

CROUCH: Well obviously, he had to make a clean breast and tell her it was all off – I mean with him going into the monastery.

ARCHIE: Quite.

CROUCH: And now he's dead. (SECRETARY *snaps her handbag shut with a sharp sound.*)

ARCHIE: A severe blow to Logic, Mr Crouch.

71

CROUCH: (*Nodding*) It makes no sense to me at all. What do you make of it, sir?

ARCHIE: The truth to us philosophers, Mr Crouch, is always an interim judgement. We will never even know for certain who did shoot McFee. Unlike mystery novels, life does not guarantee a denouement; and if it came, how would one know whether to believe it?

CROUCH: Yes, well, I'm only a caretaker, but all the same *somebody* shot him, and –

ARCHIE: A caretaker? I've been *looking* for a caretaker to take the chair at a little symposium I'm running. Are you busy this evening?

CROUCH: Me? I haven't got the qualifications.

ARCHIE: Oh, I'll give you those. Does Divinity interest you at all?

(ARCHIE *and* CROUCH *move out through the front door. The* SECRETARY *is also leaving, now wearing her* (white) *coat – which has a bright splash of blood on its back.*
GEORGE *sees the blood as she leaves the study, and the flat.*
GEORGE *realizes that the blood must have come from the top of the cupboard, i.e. wardrobe. He needs to stand on his desk or chair. He puts Pat, whom he had been holding, down now and climbs up to look into the top of the cupboard; and withdraws from the unseen depths his misfired arrow, on which is impaled Thumper. The music still continues. Holding Thumper up by the arrow,* GEORGE *puts his face against the fur. A single sob. He steps backwards, down . . . CRRRRRUNCH!!!*
He has stepped, fatally, on Pat. With one foot on the desk and one foot on Pat, GEORGE *looks down, and then puts up his head and cries out, 'Dotty! Help! Murder!'*
GEORGE *falls to the floor. The process which originally brought the set into view now goes into reverse. His last sobs are amplified and repeated right into the beginning of the Coda.*)

End of Act Two

CODA

The symposium – in bizarre dream form. CROUCH *is the Chairman.*
ARCHIE *stands to one side.*
THREE USHERS (JUMPERS) *sit in front of Crouch's raised
platform. They wear yellow gowns.*
*Stained-glass slides are in at the beginning and stay in. The sobs
subside.* GEORGE *lies still.*

CROUCH: Well, gentlemen, that's approximately two minutes of
approximate silence. I think we might proceed with our
opening statements – 'Man – good, bad or indifferent?' –
Sir Archibald Jumper.

USHER: Call Sir Archibald Jumper!

ECHO: Call Sir Archibald Jumper.

(GEORGE *remains prone. Enormous applause, unrealistically
cut off, for* ARCHIE.)

ARCHIE: Mr Crouch, ladies and gentlemen. 'Man – good, bad or
indifferent?' Indeed, if moon mad herd instinct, is God dad
the inference? – to take another point: If goons in mood, by
Gad is sin different or banned good, f'r'instance? – thirdly:
out of the ether, random nucleic acid testes or neither
universa vice, to name but one – fourthly: If the necessary
being isn't, surely mother of invention as Voltaire said, not
to mention Darwin different from the origin of the specious
– to sum up: Super, both natural and stitious, sexual ergo
cogito er go-go sometimes, as Descartes said, and who are
we? Thank you.

(*Shattering applause.*
The USHERS *hold up score cards: '9.7' – '9.9' – '9.8'.*)
Call Captain Scott!
(*Echo, echo, and an* ASTRONAUT *floats in to music.*)

CROUCH: How many witnesses do you intend to call, Sir
Archie?

ARCHIE: Three, Mr Chairman, and I shall also be making a
song and dance.

CROUCH: Oh, very well.

ARCHIE: You are Captain Scott, astronaut of no fixed abode?

SCOTT: (*Bleep.*)

CROUCH: Was that yes or no?

ARCHIE: I will ask him, Mr Crouch. Was that yes or no?

SCOTT: (*Bleep.*)

ARCHIE: Yes.

CROUCH: So long as we know. Carry on.

ARCHIE: Captain Scott, cast your mind back if you will to last Thursday morning when you and Captain Oates found yourselves on the moon. You have lately returned from there. Captain Oates has not and must be presumed late. Now, in your own words, was it not the case that pulling up the ladder was your natural response to a pure situation in a place without culture, environment or indeed history, a new-found limbo-land, a treeless Eden which made speculation fruitless?

SCOTT: (*Bleep.*)

ARCHIE: Thank you.
   (*Music.* SCOTT *floats out.*)

CROUCH: Sir Archie, are they all going to come and go in this manner?

ARCHIE: Mostly, Mr Crouch. The next one swings on. Call Lord Greystoke!

USHER: Call Lord Greystoke!

ECHO: Call Lord Greystoke.
   (TARZAN *swings in, ululating.*)

ARCHIE: You are Lord Greystoke?

GREYSTOKE: I am.

ARCHIE: It seems hardly necessary to point it out but I think I am right in saying that your father, the first Lord Greystoke, and his then-pregnant wife, Lady Alice, while sailing off the West African coast, were put ashore by a mutinous crew and left to perish in the jungle, which they did shortly after you were born, leaving you to be brought up by apes; in other words, you Tarzan.

GREYSTOKE: That is correct.

CROUCH: I suppose all this is going to lead somewhere, Sir Archie?

ARCHIE: Indeed, Mr Crouch. I have called Lord Greystoke because he is uniquely in a position to tell us whether moral values as we know them are the distinguishing marks of human nature or merely the products of civilization.

CROUCH: But isn't he a character of fiction?

ARCHIE: I will put that to him, Mr Crouch.

CROUCH: Do. I'm almost sure he's out of a book.

ARCHIE: Lord Greystoke, it has been suggested that you are out of a book.

GREYSTOKE: That is correct.

CROUCH: And the author of this book was a novelist, wasn't he?

GREYSTOKE: I have always understood him to be one's biographer.

ARCHIE: Well, you can't say fairer than that.

CROUCH: He was your creator, wasn't he?

ARCHIE: Mr Crouch, that is a cheap semantic confusion –

CROUCH: If he's a real person I'm the Archbishop of Canterbury.

ARCHIE: That is a preposterous claim – I shall be calling the Archbishop of Canterbury as my next witness.

(TARZAN *swings out of sight as the* ARCHBISHOP *enters in procession. He may be impersonated by* BONES. *There is music for the* ARCHBISHOP's *entrance. He enters, dressed as for a coronation, attended by two yellow-garbed chaplains* (JUMPERS) *who position themselves downstage, facing the audience.* GEORGE *gets to his feet and looks at* CLEGTHORPE, *who 'blesses' him.*)

USHER: (*To* ARCHBISHOP) Take the book in your right hand and read what is on the card.

ARCHBISHOP: Nine.

ARCHIE: You are Samuel Clegthorpe, Archbishop of Canterbury?

ARCHBISHOP: For my sins.

CROUCH: What does he mean by that?

ARCHIE: I think he was hoping for a Cabinet post, my lord . . . Your Grace, we are gathered together to dispute the goodness, badness or indifference of man. As the senior cleric of the Church of England, you have no doubt thought deeply about this.

CLEGTHORPE: Well, until recently, I have been mainly interested in the birds of the air and the beasts of the field – rooks, badgers, rabbits – and so on.

ARCHIE: Quite. But I think you are aware that there is great uncertainty in the land. The ground shifts. The common people look to you for guidance.

CLEGTHORPE: Yes. My chaplains had to use tear gas to disperse them. In my opinion, the Government is going too fast.
(*The* CHAPLAINS *turn to look at him.*)

ARCHIE: Surely that is a matter best left to the Government?

CLEGTHORPE: They were shouting 'Give us the blood of the lamb. Give us the bread of the body of Christ' –

ARCHIE: That's hardly a rational demand.

CLEGTHORPE: They won't go away! . . . Surely belief in man could find room for man's beliefs. . . ?
(*Behind him the* USHERS *stand up.*)

ARCHIE: Archbishop, the cat has already jumped.
(*The* USHERS *elevate* CLEGTHORPE.)

CLEGTHORPE: And there is the further question . . .
(*The* CHAPLAINS *back-flip into the middle of the stage, to join the pyramid.*)

ARCHIE: No further questions.

CLEGTHORPE: Well, I'd just like to say – I don't like to see my flock weeping in my garden at Lambeth –

ARCHIE: (*Sharply*) My Lord Archbishop, when I was last in Lambeth I saw good strawberries in your garden – I do beseech you send for some.

CLEGTHORPE: Yes, all right, but you must appreciate my position – I mean now that I *am* Archbishop of Canterbury –

ARCHIE: Will no one rid me of this copper's nark!
(*A gunshot stops the music and kills* CLEGTHORPE.)

CLEGTHORPE: George!

GEORGE: Dotty!
(*The light alters – for* DOTTY's *entrance.*)

ARCHIE: Call Dotty Moore!
(*Everything comes vividly to life: loud music brings the* JUMPERS *to their feet. The screen turns to a brilliant starry sky.*

The music is the introduction to 'Sentimental Journey', *and* DOTTY *is to make her entrance on a spangled crescent moon . . . with the* JUMPERS *as dancers.*)

JUMPERS: (*Sing*) Calling Dotty Moore, calling Dotty Moore, call Dotty Moore.

DOTTY: (*Sings*) Did I hear you call, will you tell me why?
Am I dreaming, is this really me?
Show me where to stand, and I'll tell you my
Philosophy.

Here is my consistent proposition,
Two and two make roughly four –
Gentlemen, that is my position,
Yours sincerely, Dorothy Moore.

As for man, I got my reservations,
Going by experience
Some ain't bad and some are revelations,
Never met indifference.

Heaven, how can I believe in heaven?
Just a lying rhyme for seven!
Scored for violins on multi-track
That takes me back
To happy days when I knew how to make it
I knew how to hold a tune
Till the night they had to go and break it –

GEORGE: (*Shouts*) Stop!!
(*Everything freezes.*)
A remarkable number of apparently intelligent people are baffled by the fact that a different group of apparently intelligent people profess to a knowledge of God when common sense tells *them* – the first group of apparently intelligent people – that knowledge is only a possibility in matters that can be demonstrated to be true or false, such as that the Bristol train leaves from Paddington. And yet these same apparently intelligent people, who in extreme cases

will not even admit that the Bristol train left from Paddington yesterday – which might be a malicious report or a collective trick of memory – nor that it will leave from there tomorrow – for nothing is certain – and will only agree that it did so today if they were actually there when it left – and even then only on the understanding that all the observable phenomena associated with the train leaving Paddington could equally well be accounted for by Paddington leaving the train – these same people will, nevertheless, and without any sense of inconsistency, claim to *know* that life is better than death, that love is better than hate, and that the light shining through the east window of their bloody gymnasium is more beautiful than a rotting corpse! – In evidence of which I ask you, gentlemen of the jury, to consider the testimony of such witnesses as Zeno Evil, St Thomas Augustine, Jesus Moore and my late friend the late Herr Thumper who was as innocent as a rainbow . . .

ARCHIE: Do not despair – many are happy much of the time; more eat than starve, more are healthy than sick, more curable than dying; not so many dying as dead; and one of the thieves was saved. Hell's bells and all's well – half the world is at peace with itself, and so is the other half; vast areas are unpolluted; millions of children grow up without suffering deprivation, and millions, while deprived, grow up without suffering cruelties, and millions, while deprived and cruelly treated, none the less grow up. No laughter is sad and many tears are joyful. At the graveside the undertaker doffs his top hat and impregnates the prettiest mourner.

Wham, bam, thank you Sam.

(*The light has reduced to a spot on* DOTTY.)
DOTTY: (*Sings without music*) Goodbye spoony Juney Moon.
Blackout